Mindfulness:

How to Cope with Hard Things

Adela Sandness, Ph.D.

Copyright © 2018 by **Adela Sandness**

All rights reserved. No part of this publication may be reproduced, distributed or transmitted in any form or by any means, without prior written permission.

RASA Publications
Antigonish, Nova Scotia, Canada
www.justbreatheyouareenough.com

Mindfulness: How to Cope with Hard Things/ Adela Sandness. -- 1st ed.
ISBN 978-1-9994636-0-1

Disclaimer:
The information provided in this publication, in our website or other related materials, is for your personal information only and should **not** be used to aid in any treatment or diagnosis for you, nor to supplement or replace medical, naturopathic, health or other professional advice which you should seek. Always seek the advice of your physician or other qualified health provider properly licensed to practise in the applicable health field concerning any questions you may have regarding any information obtained from this publication or related website or and any medical or health condition you believe may be relevant to you or to someone else. You agree that RASA Publications makes no representations or warranties regarding the use, functionality or efficacy of any information or advice provided. All users release RASA Publications and its personnel from all claims, liabilities and causes of action (for negligence or otherwise) in any way relating to any information provided. Please care for yourself, with honour and respect, and please be safe.

Dedication

I bow, and express gratitude and respect,
to the many teachers and students,
companions and friends
who have walked with me in my journey.
May all beings find happiness and freedom from suffering.

*"When you do something
then obstacles will come,
and you can go through them.
Obstacles are a sign of success."*

—H.H. THE 16TH KARMAPA

Contents

Preface 1

What is the Mind? 5

How to Have a Thought 29

    Step 1: Don't Believe Everything You Think 29

    Step 2: The Self is Not a Solid 41

    Step 3: Press "Pause" 50

How to Have an Emotion 57

    Step 1: You Are Stronger Than Your Fear 57

    Step 2: Apply Kindness 68

    Step 3: Give It Space 75

How to Cope With Hard Things 87

    Step 1: Look in the Mirror 87

    Step 2: Engage the Journey 108

    Step 3: Build Your Strength 127

Conclusion 133

Preface

You are enough. You have in your basic nature intelligence and resourcefulness, kindness and wisdom, insight and strength. You are sufficient. There is absence of absence. You are enough.

There is a Buddhist metaphor deeply rooted in ancient Indian cosmology which tells us that the mind is like the sun in the sky. The mind is vast like the sky. Inherent in its nature – like the sun in the sky - is kindness, wisdom and strength.

This is the nature of mind, in the same way that it is the basic nature of the body to be healthy. The body will do anything in its power to return to a state of health, because health is its basic nature. It is the basic nature of the mind to be vast, kind, flexible, resourceful, wise and strong.

The tradition holds that thou ghts are like clouds, and they can appear to be quite solid – particularly in the midst of our storms - but thoughts, like clouds, are not solid. They are not as real as they may appear, and they will come, and they will go... like clouds in the sky.

The sky is vast, and it is strong. It is able to work with the clouds as they come and they go, and so is the mind.

If I put my hand under an electron microscope, I will find that it is 99.999% space, just like the hand of any other human, every grain of sand on the beach, every star in the sky: 99.999% space.

Space is the basic nature: the nature of reality as such, the basic nature of life. In that tremendously fundamental way, it is understood to be benevolent, decent, kind, strong. It is good in a way which is so far beyond any perception of a distinction between good or bad. It is good in the way that a sunrise is good, or a plant is good.

Life itself is good, and, in that same way, you are enough. You are worthy. You are sufficient. Just like the oxygen inside of your lungs is not different from the air in the space in what appears to be outside of you, you are good by virtue of the fact that you are alive. You breathe: that's enough.

I am told that an adult human has within its body about 60% water. In the same way that the water inside of you is not fundamentally different from the water in the rivers, in the streams, and the oceans, or the water that falls from the sky, you are basically good. You are sufficient, worthy, enough in the way that water is fundamentally worthy and enough. It is life-giving. You are alive.

In this sense, mind is tremendously impersonal. Mind is impersonal in the way that the sky, or space, or oxygen is impersonal. It would be inaccurate to imagine that somehow there is someone else that is more worthy, or more enough. It would be like saying, "The mountains here on the East Coast of Canada, they are old: they are a little bit smaller; they are rounded in their shoulders. They are not like the young whippersnappers on the west coast of Canada: they're big, and tall, and spiky!".

A mountain is a mountain.

It does not shrink and try to be small in order to fit into someone else's idea of what a mountain is, or to fit into its own idea of what a better mountain should be. A mountain is a mountain, and that's enough. Gravity is gravity. Oxygen is oxygen. Alive is alive, and like all of these things, you are enough.

This is the basic nature of mind, as it would be understood in ancient Indian cosmology, or at least the roots in ancient Indian cosmology come to be understood in this way as they grow and develop into what we now describe as Buddhist psychology.

We will begin our exploration of what is a mind or a person, what is the shape of space or time, how to have a thought, how to have an emotion, and how to pick up both ends of the big sticks as we overcome hard things.

Yet our point of departure will also be our point of arrival, because it's the point: You Are Enough.

May the journey bring you joy.

Adela Sandness
Antigonish, Nova Scotia, Canada
August, 2018

Chapter 1

What is the Mind?

> *"Your heart is fully capable of expanding,
> and your mind is limitless."*
> *- Adela.*

The shape of the world, as we experience it internally as individuals, and as we experience it externally as a culture, is carved by the shape of our stories: the stories that we tell ourselves, and the stories that we are told by others. The shape of our world is, therefore, subject to change in the way that our stories, told and retold, are always subject to change.

What is the shape of the ancient Indian world? The earliest time that we know in India is the Indus Valley Civilization of about 3000 BCE. It was a high city state culture spread over a large area. They had running water, a square-block civic structure, a system of weights and measures, a system of currency. They traded with distant lands. Their art, jewelry, textiles - and in particular a style of heavily embroidered brocade - left traces and footprints in the shapes and forms that are still part of modern India.

Their dead were found in fetal position, where they had been buried with food, tools and all that they would need for a next life of some kind; it may be an early perception of reincarnation.

Objects were discovered with symbols that have continued to the modern period. There is a figure with horns that has many of the elements of the contemporary Hindu god Shiva, the great cosmic yogi. In one image, he is found seated in the bound ankle pose which is still a posture in hatha yoga practice.

There were many terra cotta Mother Goddess figures which parallel Mother Goddess images of many early cultures. They suggest honour for the fertility of life itself and an early idea of "mother India".

The Indus Valley Civilization declined, in part, as a result of geological changes that would cause some of its principal rivers to flow underground. The next phase of the roots of this ancient culture is Vedic tradition, 1500 to 500 BCE.

We can put this in context. What was happening in other places in 1500 BCE? This is about the time the Israelites were led by Moses to leave Egypt and reach Canaan, crossing the River Jordan, and Moses received the Ten Commandments on Mount Sinai. In about 1500 BCE, Troy was destroyed in the Trojan War. In Egypt, there were court dancers accompanied by harp music and regulations concerning the sale of beer. In China, they were making silk, and they had measured the height of the sun in relation to the incline of the polar axis.

1500 BCE is the time when the earliest Sanskrit texts will come into India. They had made a long journey to get there.

The earliest Sanskrit texts of the Indian subcontinent are part of what is known as Indo-European tradition. It can trace its origin back to about 10,000 BCE, at the time when humans domesticated horses. It is believed to have originated in the Steppe region of Russia. These groups of humans would begin to follow the herds on horseback. One branch of this community would follow the herds towards the west. They would come into Italy and Greece, and they would establish the ancient Greco-Roman tradition. They would continue into France, from France into England and Scotland, and they would originate Celtic tradition.

Others of them would go to the east. It is believed that they crossed the Bering Strait, would come into North America, and some First Nations peoples of North American tradition would carry this community as part of their ancestry.

There are those who would head in the direction of India. By about 5000 BCE, we speak of Indo-Iranian tradition. Among these people, some would go towards Iran and establish ancient Persian or Zoroastrian culture, and others would go into India itself, bringing with them the Sanskrit language. The earliest Sanskrit text, the Rig-Veda Samhita, is my focus of research.

The word Veda is derived from the Sanskrit verbal root VID-, which means "to know". The noun Veda thus means knowledge. It refers to sacred knowledge contained within a body of literature which is called Vedic literature. This time period in Indian history, from 1500 BCE to 500 BCE, is called the Vedic period because of the form of the Sanskrit language in which this literature is communicated.

In the same way that there is ancient Greek, classical Greek and modern Greek language, there is ancient or Vedic Sanskrit, classical Sanskrit, and the modern Indian languages of Sanskrit derivation, including, for example, Marathi, Gujarati, and Hindi.

The earliest body of Sanskrit literature, known as the Samhitas, contains poetry and hymns of praise to the gods. The second phase, about 1000 BCE, is the Brahmanas, and these are ritual manuals that were used by priests who were conducting the ceremony. It is in prose text, as opposed to poetry, and it would include several myths and stories that talk about these rituals. Late Vedic literature (c. 500 BCE) includes the Upanishads, the earliest philosophic texts of Indian tradition.

It is an oral tradition. It passed from one generation to the next in families, and from one generation to the next in master-student relationships.

There are many gods and goddesses in the Vedic pantheon. They live in what we might think of as the sky. It is a place called "devaloka", the realm of the gods. The gods are known as "devas". The word is derived from DIV- which means light. So the gods are beings of light that live in the sky. They also have shapes and forms that can be found on the earth, and in the middle region in-between the sky and the earth.

What is it to be human in this ancient Indian world view that stretches its roots far back into the deep past of human experience?

The Vedic worldview distinguishes that which is living from that which is not living. That which is living is in motion or moving. The term is "jagat". It is a noun derived from the verb GAM-, which means "to go".

I think of this sometimes, if I pause to reflect before going to the gym or doing other forms of exercise: to be alive is to be in motion. That which is not living is still. The term is "sthatar", a noun derived from STHA-, " to stand".

Inside the "jagat" class, humans have no particular distinction among other living creatures. The opposition is expressed by other characteristics such as biped – "dvipad" – as opposed to quadrupeds, the four-footed.

I used to try to explain this to my dog. I had a golden retriever, Sarah, who was my good friend for about 13 years before her transition. I explained to her that the fundamental difference between us was that humans had two hands and two feet, and therefore the opposable thumb. This permitted me to have access to the cookie jar where she did not. She was part of the class of the four-footed, without the opposable thumb and, therefore, unable to have direct access to the cookie jar in the way that I did. In many ways, this was the only real difference between us.

Two-footed, four-footed, winged ones, the ones that crawl, the ones that swim: they are parts of a whole. There was no fundamental difference between those who are alive except, for example, the distinction between two-footed ones and four-footed ones.

If that is the difference between humans and other animals, what is the distinction between humans and the gods? Humans are mortal, "martya", derived from the verb MAR-, which means "to die". They are also "jana", from JAN-, "to be born". To be human is to be born and to die.

The model for this in Vedic cosmology is that we follow the pathway of the sun. The sun comes up; the sun goes down. There is a clear beginning, middle and end. We are born, we live, and we die: the beginning and end can appear to be irrefutable.

We are born, we live, and we die. Yet, while our birth and death are limits that appear to be irrefutable, and are experienced quite sharply as real, the fact is they only appear to exist. They aren't really real. The sun comes up, the sun comes down, and the sun comes up again. The sun comes up, the sun goes down, and the sun comes up again. As human persons, we have the experience of limits that appear to be real and a quality of limitlessness simultaneously.

This is expressed in the story of two male children of the sun, sons of the sun who are ancestors, or originators, of humanity. One of these is Yama, god of the dead. His name is derived from YAM-, which means "to constrain".

We know what it feels like to be constrained: the tightness of the chest, the tightness in the forehead, the clutching of the stomach as we curl over and round down, that feeling that the limits we experience are somehow being pressed upon us: it's hard to breathe.

Death is constraint personified. He specializes in limits. Our life is a gift that comes to us from the god of the dead as if on loan, and, one day, he will take it back again.

Yama, king of the dead, rules over the ancestors. He is also king of "dharma", social responsibility. The idea of "dharma" in Hindu tradition is a continuation of the idea that, as human persons, we are born with debt. We have a debt to the gods to give offering and hymns of praise. We have a debt to the sages – the early seers and wise ones - to learn the sacred texts, their vision of sacred knowledge. We have a debt to the ancestors to have children and continue the family lineage, and we have a debt to fellow humans of hospitality.

To be born a human person in society is to be born with social responsibilities that arise as a consequence of that birth. Can we have the courage to meet those social responsibilities, as we work with the constraints of our lives?

Yet to be human is to know continuity as well as discontinuity. We have an experience of limits, but we are also able to move beyond those limits. The sun comes up; the sun goes down; the sun comes up again.

Yama has a brother named Manu. Manu is the ancestor of all humans. How is it that we are all descended from Manu? Only humans can both give and be that which is given.

This is the power and the potency of the human experience. We give of ourselves. This is how we overcome the appearance of limitations, the experience of constraint.

The story of Manu is a flood story. I know of no culture that does not have a flood story of some kind. Was it the melting of the glaciers? The fall of Atlantis? The story of Manu and the flood is told in the Shatapatha-Brahmana like this.

One day, in the morning, they brought Manu water for the washing of hands. It is the ritual cleansing of the hands that would happen before making the morning prayers, or morning offerings.

As he was pouring the water into his hands, a fish came into his hands and said, "Care for me, and I will save you". "From what will you save me?". "A flood will carry away with all these creatures. I will save you from it". "Well, how should you be cared for?". "As long as we are tiny", said the fish, "our destruction is great, for fish swallows fish". It is a common metaphor for human experience in society: big fish swallows small fish. "So, care for me at first in a pot, and, when I outgrow it, dig a trench and care for me in that. When I outgrow that, then take me down to the ocean, for then I will be beyond destruction."

So the fish grew steadily into that which grows largest, and it said, "In a certain year, the flood will come. Then you will build a ship and come to me, and when the flood has risen, you will enter the ship, and I will save you from the flood". So Manu cared for it in this way, and carried it down to the ocean.

In the very year which the fish had indicated, he built a ship and came to him. When the flood had risen, he entered the ship, and the fish swam up to him. He fastened the rope of the ship to the horn of the fish, and with it he sailed through to the northern mountain.

"I have saved you", said the fish. Fasten the ship to a tree, but do not let the water cut you off when you are on the mountain.

As the water subsides, keep following it down, and he kept following it down in this way, and so that slope of the northern mountain is known as a Manu's descent. The floods swept away all other creatures, and Manu alone remained here.

Yet Manu grew lonely in his solitude. He wished to have offspring. So he began to make offerings at the place of the fire offering. He would give offerings of food. He would give water, clarified butter or ghee, sour milk, whey and curds, and, after one year, a woman grew from these offerings. She arose quite solid, but clarified butter gathered in her footprint.

Manu said to her, "Who are you?". "I am your daughter", she replied. "How is it that you are my daughter?", he asked. She said, "Those offerings to the gods that you made - clarified butter, sour milk, whey and curds - with these things you have given birth to me. I am blessing, speech. Make use of the sacred speech that I am, and recite me while you are making these offerings. So Manu made use of the sacred speech, or mantra, that she was in the course of his offerings. With her, he went on worshipping, and giving offerings, wishing for offspring. Through her, he generated this human race, which is the race of Manu. Whatever blessing he asked for through her, all of this was granted to him.

What is it to be human? Of all the animals susceptible to be given to the gods at the place of the fire offering, only the human can both give and be that which is given.

Generosity will come to be considered the first of the "paramitas" in Buddhist tradition, the first of the "transcendent actions". How is it that we overcome the perception of difference between self and other? We give and receive with an open hand.

The sun comes up; the sun goes down; the sun comes up again, and there is a cycle of giving which mirrors this flow of our lives. For this is a world where time is round. We follow the pathway of the sun: spring, summer, fall, winter; the cycle of the seasons; the movement of the stars; the flow of our days between morning and night, morning and night; the cycle from one generation to the next.

It is elegant and poetic, the idea that time is round. It is also a demonstrable reality. The earth cycles in rotation around the sun. We call it the year. The Earth does a rotation in its axis. We call it a day.

Any ancient culture in my awareness will celebrate the cardinal and also eight directions in the wheel of the year: the winter solstice, the longest night (December 21/22), towards the spring equinox of equal night and equal day (March 21/22), towards the summer solstice (June 21/22), the longest day and shortest night, on its way to the fall equinox (September 21/22) of equal night and equal day, which will then move towards the winter solstice (December 21/22), and the wheel of the year turns again.

Time is round. It is a tremendously important part of how the old Indian stories will shape understandings of this world. In a world where time is round, the relationship between cause and effect is intimately connected. There is nowhere to go. It's a circle that can only move in the cyclical turning of its cyclical process. It's a closed system.

In my contemporary "western" culture, we talk about taking out the trash, as if there were some place for it to go. I take it out from my house. I take it to the end of a driveway. The town where I live has an infrastructure designed to pick up the trash every second Monday morning. I might think, "I have taken out the trash; it is gone", but there is nowhere for it to go. It's a closed system. In 2015, the National Geographic reported that there were 5.25 trillion pieces of plastic garbage in the ocean.

There is no such thing as "away". In a world where time is round, there is no escaping the relation between the cause and effect of the choices we make in our lives.

This flow of the life principle, following the pathway of the sun, is also the model for the cyclical movement which occurs, as we saw in the story of Manu, at the place of the fire offering.

In this old Vedic world view, humans participate in the cyclical flow of the life force through the act of giving at the place of the fire ritual. The essence of the request that is made to the gods is, "Please receive what I have to give. Please give to me what will allow me to continue to give." Please receive what I have to give. Please allow me to receive what will allow me to continue to give: physical health, strength, vitality, and children to carry on the family line. Please give me a long life. May I live one hundred winters. May I have food, and an abundance of cows, and may there be joy, and delight, and success, and humor, and satisfaction, and fulfillment."

We participate in the cycle of the flow of life by giving. With this open hand, we permit ourselves to then receive that which will allow us to continue to give. We overcome the perception of limitation through this act of giving, participating in the flow of the life force, and this connecting to a life principle as such brings us joy.

This cyclical flow of the life force between heaven and earth, and the way in which humans are part of that cycle, is closely connected with the Indian idea of reincarnation. The sun comes up, the sun goes down, the sun comes up again. In this flow of the lifeforce, "we flow together". This is a literal rendering into English of the Sanskrit term "samsara": we flow together.

What is the relationship between our inside worlds and our outside worlds? The water inside of me, and the water in the ocean is a same water. The oxygen in my lungs and the oxygen in the air is a same oxygen. How do I relate to my environment? How am I part of that whole?

We hear this described in the early funeral hymns in Rig-Veda Book 10. The poet addresses the one newly dead saying:

"May your eye go to the sun, your life's breath to the wind. Go to the sky or to earth, as is your nature; or go to the waters, if that is your fate. Take root in the plants with your limbs.

Set him free again to go to the ancestors, [O cremation fire god Agni] when he has been offered to you as an offering and wonders with the sacrificial [offering] drink. Let him reach his own descendants [which is to say, let him be reborn in the line of his own descendants], dressing him in a lifespan. O knower of creatures, let him join with a body."

In this search for a new body, the one who is newly dead follows a path. This path has been traced for him by Yama, god of the dead, and crossed by the first ancestors. Yama has two dogs who guard this path.

The description of this path is further developed in a late Vedic text called the Brihad-Aranyaka-Upanishad. In its description of death and rebirth, the text is somewhat explicit, so please forgive me if you find it immodest. From the Brihad-Aranyaka-Upanishad 6.2:

(13) Woman, in truth, is like fire. Her womb is the fuel, her hair the smoke, the vulva the flame, that which is introduced the charcoal, the pleasure the stars. In this fire, the gods offer sperm; from this offering is born the man.

He lives what he lives. When he dies

(14) one takes him to the [crematory] fire [the god Agni]. His fire is the fire, the fuel the fuel, the smoke the smoke, the flame the flame, the charcoal the charcoal, the stars the stars. In this fire, the gods offer the man; from this offering is born this man resplendent in radiance.

(16) As for those who conquer the worlds (who make offerings), they enter the smoke, from the smoke into the night, from the night into the fifteen dark days of the moon, from the fifteen dark days into the six months that the sun goes towards the south, from these months into the world of the ancestors, from the world of the ancestors into the moon; when they have attained the moon they become food, and this the gods eat following the increasing and decreasing of the rhythm of the king Soma. When this step is finished for them, they re-enter space, from space into the air, from the air into the rain, from the rain into the earth; returned to the earth, they become food; thus again they are offered into the fire that is the man, and,

from there, reborn into the fire that is the woman. Thus, climbing again into various places, they follow the cycle."

We are part of a whole. We will feel satisfaction, fulfillment and a wholeness to the degree that we experience a connection with that wholeness of which we are a part.

So what is the nature of mind as understood in ancient Indian tradition? What do we most need to hear in these stories that were told to help us give shape, and meaning, and purpose to our lives?

One of the stories most beautiful to me, because of its transparent and elegant simplicity, is the story of the creation of the world from a golden egg. It looks like an egg, doesn't it? Look out onto the horizon, the curve of the sky that meets the flat of the earth. It's an egg!

"There once was an egg. It floated on an ocean that existed in the time before time. It moved, and it opened, and the top became the sky, and the bottom became the earth, and the space in-between became the atmospheric realm in which we all live."

There's so much for us to hear in this story. Let's begin with the space in-between. It is a most precious thing for us to learn about how ancient India shaped and understood our world.

Many of us are familiar with the work of Mohandas K. Gandhi. Gandhi was a leader in modern India as it sought to end colonial rule by the British Empire. The model of how he did this would inspire Nelson Mandela, and Martin Luther King, as they also worked to decolonise.

Why did Gandhi win? He won because he was not fighting. Gandhi understood the potential of the space in-between. We find it in the philosophic principle of non-dualism: we win because we're not fighting back. The model of the space in-between reminds us that there are ways of seeing the world that are not, by their nature, confrontational or oppositional like two clapping hands.

Some worldviews are dualistic. Let me offer an example of a creation story that is shaping a world in relation to ideas that are dualistic, in order that we may better understand this idea of non-dualism by the contrast. It is not to say one is better than the other. It is not to say that one is either good or bad, but it is to say that it is possible to shape a world where things are neither good nor bad. This is an example of non-dualism.

If we turn with respect to the Genesis creation stories, time is a line. The days unfold in linear succession. In the beginning, God created the heaven and the earth. Darkness was upon the face of the earth. God said, "Let there be light", and there was light. God saw the light was good. God divided the light from the darkness. God called the light day, the darkness night. The evening and the morning were the first day.

We have the heavens and the earth, the night and the day, woman and man: it is a series of opposites. The sense that it is either this or that can lead to an experience of living in a world that is oppositional: either one or the other, either inside or outside, either part of our group or outside of our group, either male or female. You are either for me, or you are against me.

It's a series of opposites. It can lead to a style of thinking that doesn't know how to move outside or beyond this oppositional, binary, quality. It can be constrained especially for those who don't identify with either this side or that side. It can feel constrained, if we don't know how to step outside of a polarized style of thinking and explore stepping into a "space in-between".

Gandhi won because, among other things, he was not fighting. To use his expression, "an eye for an eye makes the whole world blind". No one wins a war. If I think about contemporary conversations that are happening about nonbinary gender, for example, I feel there are people who are inspired to explore the possibility that there is a space in-between. Neither this nor that; both this and that; not just black and white, but the wonder and delight of a full spectrum of possibilities: there is much to discover in this intellectual view of non-dualism.

It's one of the great gifts of exploring other people's world views. It shows us that there are many, many different ways of dreaming a world. It creates space and opportunity for us to explore other ways of dreaming our own, whether it's the individual world or that of our larger community. I feel it lacks humility to say so, but I really do agree with Einstein: we will not solve our problems using the same style of thinking we were using when we created them. What would it be like to step into a space in-between, and a style of thinking where things are neither good nor bad, or it's possible to be both right and wrong?

It's the space in-between in which we all live. That space, between heaven and earth, is where life is.

Now, what is the story telling us about structure? What is it saying about limitation? The top became the sky; the bottom became the earth. Because there is the structure of the sky and the earth - because there are these clear limits - there is, therefore, a space in-between.

We are humans because we are born and we die. The great limit for the individual is that space in-between birth and death. How is it that sometimes we think we're going to live forever?

How many of us know someone who, at some point, was given a fatal diagnosis: they were told by a medical professional, "I'm so very sorry. This will kill you. I'm so very sorry; you're going to die." Maybe it was a cancer diagnosis. If it's you who received this diagnosis, I'm so very, very sorry for your suffering.

For me, someone said this at 4:45 on a Friday afternoon: "I'm so very sorry this could kill you. We did not expect this test result. I'm so very sorry that this could kill you."

The people that you know who have gone through this experience, did they somehow become more alive knowing that their time left was limited? ....knowing that one must seize the day, and live now, because our days are numbered?

I will try to save you the suffering of 4:45 on a Friday afternoon. I will just tell you: we are all going to die. By virtue of the fact that we are born, we are all going to die.

You, too, one day will die. You have permission to live now.

It is a finite experience, the course of a single, individual lifetime. It does have a beginning, middle and end, like the cyclical flow of the sun through the sky. Morning to night; morning to night; morning to night: it is said that our days are counted like so many beads on a string of prayer beads, like the 108 beads on a Hindu or Buddhist mala.

The number represents infinity. We are parts of a whole. We are connected with the life principle itself, but in this individual experience of this body, and this human lifetime, my days are counted off one after the other like so many beads on a prayer string.

It is a gift in my live – in anyone's life - to know that it has limits. It can be an inspiration to rise up and meet that bar.

There was a time when I was working quite regularly with a trainer at a gym. One of my favorite machines at the gym was the "lat pull down". You sit on the bench, and you reach up to the bar, and you pull down the weight. To do it properly, one contracts the muscles of the back while it's happening. This necessarily has the effect of opening the chest. The strength comes because there is an open heart, and then we lift the chest and rise up to meet that bar.

If the ultimate limit is our death, and it feels like we're spending our lives banging into obstacles, we can remember, as we flow together through our nights and our days, that the flow of our life is like a river. It is life-giving because there is structure. Because there is limit, we are able to stretch, and grow, and overcome it.

We are finite and infinite simultaneously. We grow stronger when we find our edge and meet the bar.

Perhaps the most important thing for us to see in this story is that, while it may feel like our world is in bits and pieces from time to time, we are, in fact, part of a whole. That wholeness does not go anywhere. There is nowhere that it can go.

There was a golden egg - it looks just like the sun - and it's floating on the horizon of the ocean. It moves. It opens. The top came the sky, and the bottom became the earth, and the space in between became the atmospheric realm in which we all live.

It's still floating on the ocean. The ocean didn't go anywhere.

The separateness that is the parts of the whole appears but is not really real. There is a substratum, or foundation of existence, that is portrayed here as our primordial ocean, the ocean that existed in the time before time. It sustains us. It supports us. We are floating and held by it, even if it is not something that we feel consciously. There is a life principle as such that flows through us, and indeed is us, in the same way that the water inside my body, and the water inside the ocean, is a same water.

We – like all parts of the whole - are mirrors, one to the other. People of Vedic tradition would understand that there is an ocean on the earth, the earthly ocean, but there is also a sky ocean. Otherwise it wouldn't be blue! Of course it's an ocean! Then there's the ocean of the space in-between: if it wasn't an ocean, where would rain come from?

Within the human, there is an ocean of the heart. The life principle, as such, contained in this primordial ocean, is the life principle contained in our earthly ocean, the ocean that is the sky, the ocean that is the space in between, and the ocean of the heart: it is a life principle as such from which life arises without itself living.

We are born from the waters. An ancient Indo-European story that tells us that all of creation comes from the churning of the ocean, the churning of the waters, in the same way that butter is churned from milk. The most concrete example is embryonic womb water. Water is part of any human birth; we are born from the waters. The water inside of me, the water outside of me, the water in any person, the water in my environment, the water as it existed at any point in time and also beyond time, is a same water symbolizing the life principle as such, worthy of honor, dignity and respect because it is life itself.

It is in me. It is of me. It is perhaps the most real thing about me, from a certain point of view, and yet I do not own it. I have it, but I don't really possess it. My life is just given me by the god of the dead on loan. What part of it is actually mine? What about it is really me in a way that separates me from any other being that lives because of water?

We are part of a whole, and we feel fulfilled and satisfied to the degree that we connect to that wholeness of which we are a part. Here differences and distinctions appear but are not really real.

Among the classical schools of Hindu philosophy is Advaita Vedanta. It is rooted in non-dualism. For them there is a life principle as such: that from which life arises without itself living. It is impersonal: not this and not that. The Brihad-Aranyaka-Upanishad describes it as, "not course not fine; not short, not long; not glowing like fire; not adhesive like water. It has no shadow, no darkness. It is without air and without space. It is without stickiness, odorless, tasteless. It has no eye, no ear, no voice, no wind. It is without breath, without mouth, without fear, without measure. It has no inside, no outside: it consumes nothing whatsoever, and nothing whatsoever consumes it. Yet, at the command of that life principle, the sun and moon stand apart. At the command of that life principle, the earth and the skies stand apart. At the command of that life principle, the moments, the hours, the days, the nights, the fortnights, the months, the seasons, the years stand apart. At the command of that life principle, some rivers flow from the snowy mountains to the east, others to the west, in whatever direction each flows."

When it is experienced as outside the individual self, they call that life principle "Brahman". When it is experienced as inside the individual self, they call that life principle "Atman".

In the same way that the ocean in my heart, the ocean of the earth, the ocean of the sky, and the ocean of the space in-between are all ocean: there is no difference. In that way, when I realize that water is just water, life is just life, Atman is Brahman – there is no difference – I will have attained "moksha", a Hindu perception of enlightenment.

The ancient text that I work on, the Rig-Veda Samhita, distinguishes between "the world of form", the world of shapes and colors that can be perceived by the external senses, and a transcendent world beyond that "world of form". There is a reality that we perceive with the external senses that appears but which is distinct from "absolute reality", or reality as such. That which appears and is perceptible by the external senses looks real, but in fact, it is just a reflection floating on the surface: like the top and the bottom and the space in-between of our egg. It is simultaneously whole and in parts. It is sustained and held up by the deep substratum of life itself that is the waters. It is no more different from that water than the wave to the sea.

Both Hindus and Buddhists name this appearance of separateness that we experience with the external senses "maya". It is derived from MA-, "to measure". That which is measurable is finite; it is "finitude". It develops the idea of Yama, god of the dead, as "constraint". It reflects the appearance of limit as the sun comes up and down, giving us our life by giving us the appearance of distinct and separate finite days. Our limits appear, but they are not really real. To see through the illusion of "maya" is another way of describing enlightenment in both Hindu and Buddhist traditions.

If Hinduism will especially appreciate the metaphor of water for the life principle itself - sacred and worthy of honor, dignity and respect - Buddhism will appreciate the vastness of space, both within and beyond the appearance of limits that is the world of form.

The mind is vast like the sky. Our life force will increase when we taste that space enough to remember this vastness. Increasing the space in our lives is part of what we accomplish through mindfulness practice. My hand under an electron microscope, just like any other hand, will show itself as 99.999% space, just like every grain of sand and every star in the sky.

In Buddhist tradition, this distinction between the "world of forms", of color and shape perceptible by the external senses – like the limits defined by the seemingly separate parts of our golden egg – is considered "relative reality". It appears to float just on the surface of an "absolute reality", an aspect of mind accessible beyond the limits of our external senses, beyond the conceptual mind that understands things in shape, and colour, and form.

The nature of mind is space as such: vast like the sky, life-giving like oxygen, and impersonal in the way that water or gravity are not personal. Mind is just mind.

Sanskrit words for "mind" tend to locate it in the heart center. So, by "mind" we mean a vast sense of the term: that which knows, that which is aware. It is identified with space itself. Its inherent qualities are infinitely accessible.

It is compassionate and kind, intelligent and wise, resourceful and strong. It has nothing to prove. There is no territory to defend. It is inherently abundant, inherently sufficient. There is an absence of absence. It is utterly enough. To connect to this quality of mind is to connect to what we already are: 99.999% space, accessible to us with every breath.

Remember how to taste and relax into that, and we will find satisfaction, fulfillment, achievement, creativity, friendship, love, humor and delight. For these are part of the expression of reality as such, this primordial quality of space that is the nature of what we are. It is a basic Buddhist understanding of mind: your heart is fully capable of expanding and your mind is limitless.

Chapter 2

How to Have a Thought

*"Often, we are 'had' by our thoughts.
Make it the other way around."*
-Adela.

Step 1: Don't Believe Everything You Think

The story of the golden egg floating on the primordial ocean is an early image of how Buddhist psychology would come to understand the nature of mind. The mind itself is stable and strong and is a foundation of our existence, like space; it feels a good deal like the primordial quality of these waters. This is the genuine nature of mind, sometimes called "absolute reality". When our mind is able to relax into this space, and recognize that as being its origin and home, then we bring into our lives contentment, satisfaction, fulfillment, creativity, achievement, friendship and delight.

There is another part of the mind which floats, as it were, on the surface. Like the golden egg, it gives us our life and our death, with its edges and limits. It is an aspect of the mind which is constructed. It is a part of us that can feel like it's in bits and pieces, and it is the conceptual, or thinking, mind.

The conceptual, thinking mind is able to perceive and understand what is called "relative reality". This is our everyday existence of the comings and the goings. I can have a conversation with you because I perceive myself as a person having a conversation with you as a person: because I see us as being separate, we are able to have a relationship. Because I understand that I have a hand, and that it is able to hold the tea cup - which I see as separate from the hand - I am able to have a cup of tea and enjoy that. This is working with the conceptual mind that understands relative reality based on the information that it is able to perceive and process from the external sensory perceptions.

Those of you who are "Star Trek: The Next Generation" fans might be familiar with the show's character, Geordi La Forge. Geordi La Forge, the show tells us, was born blind. So he wears what he calls a visor. The visor is very fancy 24th century technology. The visor is able to perceive a vast amount of information that would far exceed what Geordi would be able to process. So the visor is able to condense that information and filter it, as it were, so it comes to Geordi in a way that Geordi is able to receive it.

Like Geordi's visor, our sensory perceptions are our gateway to the outside world. Eyes, ears, nose, tongue, touch: all of these are actually able to perceive much more information than we are able to process. The conceptual mind supports our day to day functioning by being that filter that permits us to receive information from the outside world through the sensory perceptions.

So what information do we receive, and what information is filtered out? This can often get us in trouble: knowing how we get in trouble goes a long way to helping us to get out again.

The conceptual mind is only able to perceive or receive information for which it has a pre-existing concept. It's like only being able to file a piece of paper if we already have a labelled folder for that piece of paper in the filing cabinet. Any information, or any piece of paper that doesn't have a corresponding folder already in the filing cabinet, will naturally be filtered out. So the conceptual mind is conditioned and constructed. We have folders in the filing cabinet because of our past experiences or our past behaviors.

Let me give an historic example. Charles Darwin, who invented the theory of evolution, sailed around the world in a large ship known as the "Beagle". He studied birds, for example, in many places, including the Galapagos Islands. He was a careful and accurate observer. He found that when the "Beagle" was anchored on the horizon line near the Islands, the people born on the Islands were not able to "see" the ship even when it was pointed out to them. They could see the small row boats taking people from the ship to the Islands: these boats were about the size of their own canoes. They could not see anything on the horizon that they were being told was a "ship", however. They could not conceive that a boat could be that big, so they were physically not able to see it.

Information that has no corresponding pre-existing concept will be filtered out by the conceptual mind.

It is possible that what we said earlier about the nature of mind didn't match a pre-existing concept that you might have about yourself. In case it is useful, let me repeat: you are fundamentally worthy. You merit dignity and respect. You have basic resourcefulness. You can determine what it is that you need and respond to that need in an appropriate and good way. You have basic intelligence, and, like the nature of mind itself - that underlying basic nature of mind that they would call "absolute reality" - you are, by your nature, both kind and wise. It is, therefore, utterly and completely possible for us to reach into ourselves, to reach into our experience of a relationship with another person, to reach into any situation or circumstance, and to draw out these inherent qualities and characteristics.

Anything that we don't believe about ourselves or other people, anything that doesn't match our idea of ourselves or other people, can be filtered out. In a sense, that we don't believe it makes it not real, for us.

So, in case it is useful, let me offer: any human body is utterly and absolutely beautiful. The body itself, as part of the planet herself, can only be utterly and absolutely beautiful. Just because you might not believe it, doesn't mean it's not true.

Don't believe everything you think.

This filtering quality of the conceptual mind can lead us to do something that is called "confusing the general and the specific". The information that we receive is filtered by our pre-existing concept: our pre-existing concept is established by our past experience.

In a sense, we're only able to see that which we expect to see, or to put ourselves in situations where we will be treated in the way that we expect to be treated.

So let me offer another historic example. There was a time, once upon a time, when I was an undergraduate student, and I was sharing a house with other undergraduate students. Now, this was the deep and ancient past, when dinosaurs roamed and computer printing paper came in very large pieces, as a perforated single sheet, that had perforated holes along both sides. It is one of the evolutions of technology where I sometimes wonder if what we lost was more than what we gained, because that computer paper made the most perfect wallpaper.

Those of us who lived in the house took some of that paper and used it as wallpaper to paper a downstairs bathroom. This made it very convenient for us to write graffiti when using the downstairs bathroom. There was a particular graffiti art - in a prime location in the downstairs bathroom - which carried the title, "Men we know who are not pigs". As the year went on, it came to pass that several of those names would be struck off the list, as the women in the house concluded, effectively, "all men are pigs".

For the sake of gender equity, let me add that surely somewhere in a house, just down the road, there were men, who were living together sharing a house, who also had determined that this was excellent paper to use to wallpaper a bathroom, and the list in their bathroom read something like, "Women we know who are not bitches". Perhaps, as was our case, it was a very short list and tended to lead to the general conclusion, "all women are bitches".

We don't actually need to use historic examples in order to illustrate this confusing of the general and the specific. We all know men who have been so badly hurt in relationship that they are left feeling, "If one woman could hurt me like that, all women could hurt me like that", and it becomes hard to engage in any relationship. If it happened once, surely it could happen again.

We all know women who have been hurt in relationship; perhaps it's a situation of violence. If one man could treat her like that, then any man could treat her like that, and it's very hard to engage in relationship with any man.

It becomes understood by the mind, "Men are like that". "Women are like that." It's how we establish a general concept, and it's a very fundamental way that the mind permits us to protect ourselves, seeking to help us to be safe.

The mind can become so conditioned by its experience, however, that repeating the behaviour becomes all that it is able to do. Sometimes the mind concludes that "all men", "all women" are "like that" so much that all a person is able to see – to not filter out - is the next someone who will continue the same behavioral pattern in the next relationship. My examples are heterosexual examples, but I observe that any human can risk to cause harm to any other human in a relationship, and that harm can become generalized by anyone.

There are surely many women, and many men, who have behaved badly. We are, strictly speaking, animals, capable of predatory behaviour. I have learned, however, since those undergraduate days: not all men are pigs.

There are many, many, many of us all – in my observation – who have, and who foster, the courage to be kind. This is our basic nature. The rest is an exception: it makes the news because it is an exception.

Kindness is our basic nature in the way that space is basic in the room, or car, or wherever you are with me at the moment. It is so basic, we forget how to see it. You will remember how to see it, however, the next time someone holds a door open for you, or the next time a store clerk tells you to have a nice day.

The ability to recognize this "confusion of the general and the specific" is helpful not only in personal contexts, but also when one is in a leadership position working with institutional dynamics. When is a person actually having a conversation with me? When is a person "filling in the blanks" and interacting instead with their concept of the role that I am filling in my workplace - "boss" - treating me in a way that has nothing to do with me as an individual person or me in this specific situation? We don't need to take it personally. We all wear visors.

The ability of the conceptional mind to see only what it expects to see can also lead us to express behavioral patterns such as racism or sexism. There would be children in our local First Nations community who would be frightened of me because I'm white. They have learned with good reason that, "all white people are frightening".

Similarly, I had a conversation recently with one of the student leaders in our campus Students' Union. I learned that the phenomenon still exists, even in a generation after mine: a woman can sit in a meeting and say something, and there is absolute silence. A man can then repeat the exact same thing, about two minutes later, and suddenly the room delights: that is such a wonderful idea that he just had! It can sometimes be a conscious intent to cause harm to the woman in the room, but often enough it's simply that they have filtered her out: they honestly are not able to hear what she's saying because they have a concept of her as female and therefore deprive her of presence or authority.

Over time, with effort, patience, and enough repeat specific information, "their" concept of "women" may adapt and change. There is, however, often no need to take it personally. Most characteristic, perhaps, is condescending behaviour by either women or men needing to diminish another person. Don't take it personally.

Remember, you are not limited by someone else's concept of you. You are limited only by your concept of yourself.

Their concept of you is a reflection of them. Your concept of you is a reflection of you.

Your concept of you is constantly subject to change. As you connect more and more with the limitless quality of the mind, your potential as a person increasingly becomes limitless.

So the conceptual mind will receive only information that conforms to its previously established patterns of thinking. How do these patterns of thinking become established?

These patterns of thinking, and behavior, are established as a result of past action or past experience. They inter-connect with the Buddhist perception of "karma". In fact, sometimes these habitual patterns are called "karmic momentum": once we've done something once, it becomes easier to do it a second time. It eventually forms a habit, so that the action begins, in a sense, to "do itself, by itself" without my consciously paying attention to it. In a world where time is round, karmic momentum is understood to move with us from one lifetime to the next.

"Karma", the noun is derived from the Sanskrit verbal root KR-, "to do"; it means simply "action". As humans, by nature we act. We are part of the class "jagat": we act - we move - because we are alive. "Karma" is neither good nor bad in its inherent nature. It's tremendously neutral in the way that gravity is neutral, but it does understand that the fruit is inside of the seed - that we will pick up both ends of a stick simultaneously - and there is no getting away from the fact that every action will have an equal and like reaction.

Much of mindfulness practice is designed to support us in becoming aware of our "habitual patterns". What patterns of thinking, or patterns of behavior, are unfolding in our lives or our experience, outside of our awareness, because they are so habitual that we are not able to see what it is that we are doing or to understand that we would have other options?

Mindfulness practice is designed to help us to let go of these habits, to drop these habitual patterns of thinking or behavior. It's understood that to drop our "big sticks" - to let go of the things that can define limits for ourselves that aren't really real - is helpful and useful. It will increase our sense of opportunity, possibility, freedom and delight. It is a way of helping ourselves to have more space in how we relate to ourselves and our world.

So let me offer that a "complete karmic act", as it relates to the actor, has three parts. First, there is the intention to act. Then there is the action itself. Then there is a feeling of satisfaction that the action has taken place (like the satisfaction of revenge, for example) and the corresponding absence of regret.

The feeling of sincere regret is understood to be part of the way that we can let go of memories, or behaviors, or patterns that are "not skillful" in the sense that they cause harm to ourselves or other people.

In Buddhist monastic tradition, regret is practiced at every full and new moon cycle through a practice called "sojong". It's a practice established by the historic Buddha himself. It is a ritual or ceremonial cleansing, an opportunity to practice active regret and let go of those things that are holding us back or weighing us down.

Once every two weeks, there is a day to give pause and ask myself, "What am I feeling badly about?". "What am I feeling frustrated about?". "What do I regret?". "Is there someone I feel like I've hurt?". "What do I need to do to set things right?". Once every two weeks, at the new and full moon, is the day to set things right, to have those difficult conversations so things don't get harder and heavier because they are left unsaid.

There's time for personal contemplation. There's time for group contemplation, and then it's time to freshly shave one's head, to put on a clean set of robes, to ritually have the fresh start - the reboot and letting go - as we then move through the next two week moon cycle.

Can we be brave enough to let go? Can we be brave enough to let go of part of our experience of ourselves, and therefore part of our identity, letting go of what limits us in order that we can access more of this space that will increase our joy and delight?

This tradition ritually provides space to give opportunity for us to regret, and to let go of things that are weighing us down and holding us back. I am told that guilt was very much not a part of this historic tradition. When the Dalai Lama first came to the west and began to teach to "westerners", he was asked a question that he did not understand. He had to ask his translator to explain, and this more than one time. He needed to be directly told by his translators what "guilt" is. It is said that he was genuinely surprised. Do you mean to tell me that there are people in this room who walk around feeling badly about themselves, and somehow have the sense that they could be basically bad and fundamentally unworthy? This made no sense to him because it was not part, we are told, of the culture where he himself was raised.

Tibetan culture has the idea that the human birth is precious. It is a rare and remarkable opportunity for a being to progress on the spiritual path. If one is born in the god realm, the time between cause and effect is so long that it is difficult to learn anything: paradise is lovely but not an effective teaching situation. If one is born in the animal realm, the self-awareness available makes it difficult to evolve on the spiritual path. The human birth is perfect because it is the space in-between.

I could have reincarnated as a mosquito, or an ant…perhaps an amoeba. Odds are statistically much greater. So how precious is the human birth?

There are old stories that seek to describe this. One old story has been adapted to the technology of our modern period. It says the odds of being granted a human birth are the odds of what it would be like to take a needle, and put it in the ground in the middle of an open field of grasses. Then, take a single green pea, go into an airplane, and fly that airplane fly way up above the cloud line. Once we are above the clouds, and we have that single green pea in our hands, we reach out through the window, and we drop the pea from the sky. It lands exactly on that needle that we've put into the ground, and it stays there. What are the odds of that?

That's how precious the human birth is. Why? Because as humans we have enough self-awareness that we can grow in our ability to understand the thinking patterns of the mind as being patterns of the mind, and we can allow ourselves to have the freedom that comes from letting go.

A well-known passage by the 14th century Tibetan Buddhist master Tsongkhapa reads:

"This human birth is precious, our opportunity to awaken. The body is impermanent, and time of death is uncertain. The cause and effect of karma shapes the course of our lives. Life has inevitable difficulties. No one can control it all. This life we must know as the tiny splash of a raindrop, a thing of beauty that disappears even as it comes into being. Therefore, I recall my inspiration and my aspiration [to engage the spiritual path] and resolve to make use of every day and night to realise it."

Step 2: The Self is Not a Solid

Step two is to experiment with the possibility that "the self is not a solid". That which we perceive and experience as being "ourselves" is quite demonstrably fluid and changing all the time.

My best Halloween costume ever happened, well, probably longer ago than I want to remember now. It was during a time that I had a kind of a gap year, I suppose, between my university degrees, and I was working full time at a non-profit organization that was providing AIDS education and support to people who were HIV positive or with AIDS in their families: an AIDS service organization. I was the only heterosexual on the block, as it were, in that group of people, and I had all kinds of opportunity to make friends with various different people who were drag queens.

That particular Halloween, one of my friends who was a drag queen did my makeup with the kind of makeup that he would know how to do, with the kind of eyelashes that he would know how to do, and the artificial fingernails that he would know how to do. I think I did have my own hair, but I think he made it much larger than it usually was. I happened to have a very heavy emerald silk long, flowing gown that I had brought back from India some years before.

I went to a church fundraiser, and I did tarot card readings. They weren't really tarot cards; they were angel cards. Do you know angel cards? You pull a card, and it will say something like "appreciation" or "gratitude". I read cards for children at this Halloween church fundraiser.

They would come in through the door: there was a silk curtain on the door, and there was very gypsy-like atmospheric lighting. I had crystals on a piece of silk on the table, and the children would come in – one at a time. They would sit down - they were four, six, maybe seven years old - and I would say to them, "My name is Sophia. I was born in Yugoslavia, and it is there that I was raised by wolves." They would hear their card reading: the angel card might say something like "kindness", so I would say to them something about kindness. Then they would get up with their eyes all big and round, and they would go out to their parents waiting on the other side of the curtain, and they would say: "She was raised by wolves!". I did readings for some of the parents, too. Even some of them were rather taken aback and wide-eyed by Sophia.

Selves shift and change all the time. We can get chased by our wolves, if we fail to see it. Let me tell you another wolf story.

There was a Buddhist teacher who was also a marathon runner. He would often go running in the woods. Maybe it was early in the morning, in that time between night and day, when the sun hasn't risen yet, and the occasional bird is singing, but it sounds somewhat out of place, or maybe it was evening when the moon is casting shadows.

He would go running in the woods, but he didn't go running in the woods alone. He would go accompanied by maybe two or three other people. So one day...I think I'll make it morning...I love that time between about 4:00 and 6:00 in the morning....one morning, he was running through the woods accompanied by two or three other people. Ahead of them -unexpectedly, unimaginably – there was, standing there alone: a wolf. They all stopped.

In principle, the men who were with him were there to protect him, but I am told they all had the instinct to look to him as if to ask: now what do we do? They stood...still... and they watched, and they waited. What would the wolf do? Their hearts were pounding. They were sweating in their palms. They had all the physical responses of being there looking eye to eye with a wolf, until they realised that the wolf had not moved for quite some time. They took a step closer. They took a step closer, and suddenly they realized: "wolflessness". It wasn't a wolf. There was never a wolf there in the first place. It was just an oddly-shaped stone hard to see in the shadows of the half-light.

They realised "wolflessness". There was never a wolf there in the first place. They only related to it as if it were real, as if it were solid, when, in fact, it was not.

The Sanskrit word that is used in Buddhist tradition, that it is rendered in English as "enlightenment", is the word "nirvana". The word "nirvana", means "extinction". It's extinction, in the way that we might extinguish a candle. A candle is extinguished, and the flame is gone. To extinguish our perception that the self exists; to extinguish our perception of a self; to allow the mind to utterly, and fully, and completely relax into its inherent nature that is space: extinguishing the idea of a self is how Buddhists would understand "enlightenment".

There was never a self there in the first place.

One of the ways we can get ourselves in trouble, and increase our suffering, is the act of trying to make the self, real, solid, permanent and unchanging when, in fact, it simply is not. The self is not a solid.

Several stories from Buddhist tradition will both explore and illustrate this understanding that the self is made of composite parts. One of these more well-known stories is a record of a conversation with a Greek king whose name was Menander. He ruled in northwest India about the middle of the second century: he was converted to Buddhism by a monk whose name was Nagasena.

One day, we are told, the King Menander went up to the Venerable Nagasena, greeted him respectfully, and sat down. Nagasena replied to the greeting, the king was pleased, and the King Menander asked, "How is your Reverence known? What is your name?" "I'm known as Nagasena, Your Majesty. That's what my fellow monks call me, but although my parents may have given me such a name, it's really only a generally understood term...a practical designation. There's no question of a permanent individual implied in the use of the word". "Listen, you five hundred Greeks and eight thousand months!", said King Menander. "This Nagasena has just declared that there is no permanent individuality implied in his name!". Then, turning to Nagasena, he said, "If, Reverand Nagasena, there is no permanent individuality, who gives you monks your robes and food, lodging and medicines? And who makes use of them? Who lives a life of righteousness, meditates, and reaches nirvana? Who destroys living beings, steals, fornicates, tells lies or drinks spirits? If what is said is true there is neither merit nor demerit; there is neither cause nor effect of action. If someone were to kill you, there would be no question of murder. There would be no masters, no teachers, no Buddhist order, and no ordinations. If your fellow monks call you Nagasena, what then is Nagasena? Would you say that your hair is Nagasena?" "No, Your Majesty." "Or your nails, teeth, skin, or other parts of your body? Are any of these Nagasena?". "No, Your Majesty." "Then are all these taken together Nagasena?". "No, Your Majesty?". "Or anything other than they?". "No, Your Majesty". "Then, for all my asking, I find no Nagasena. Nagasena is a mere sound. Surely what Your Reverence has said is false.

Then the Venerable Nagasena addressed the king, "Your Majesty, how did you come here - on foot or in a vehicle?". "In a chariot". "Tell me, what is the chariot?". "Is the pole the chariot?".

"No, Your Reverence." "Or the axle, wheels, frame or the reins for the horses? The yoke for the horses? Are any of these the chariot?". "None of these is the chariot." Then all these separate parts taken together, are they the chariot?". "No, Your Reverence." "Then is the chariot something other than the separate parts?". "No, Your Reverence". "Then for all my asking, Your Majesty, I can find no chariot: that chariot is a mere sound. What then is the chariot? Surely what Your Majesty has said is false! There is no chariot!"

When he had spoken, the five hundred Greeks cried, "Well done!", and said to the king, "Now Your Majesty. Get out of that dilemma if you can!". "What I said was not false," replied the king. "It is on the account of all these various components - the pole, the axle, the wheels and so on - that the vehicle is called a chariot. It's just a generally understood term, a practical designation." "Well said, Your Majesty! You know what the word chariot means, and so it is just the same with me. It's on account of the various components of my being that I am known by the generally understood term, the practical designation, Nagasena."

What am I? Am I my hair, my eyebrows, my finger nails, my toe nail polish? If I change my finger or toe nail polish, am I no longer me? Am I my arms and legs? If I were to lose these, am I somehow less me? What about my thoughts? My feelings? These change all the time: when they come and go, am I somehow less me? Perhaps my goals, my dreams, my friends, my loves? As they come and go, am I somehow less me? Where is this me? "Me" is constantly changing. There is no permanent, solid self that I can call "me".

I am an idea. I am a concept that I imagine to be myself. Like the wolf in the woods, it looks like a "self", but it is not really real.

"I" am a concept understood by my conceptual mind. How my conceptual mind understands "me" tends to limit possibilities that would otherwise be right there for me, if my concept of self were able to be more flexible, more open, more relaxed. Ideas, including the idea "me", are all subject to change: we just need to tell different stories.

This is part of what is being offered by the mindfulness practices. Can we gradually let go of this thing that we think of as a "self"? Can we gradually come to understand that there is nothing to prove, and there is no territory to defend? There are various ways that Buddhist tradition will seek to help us to relax the idea of the self by showing the self to be made of composite parts, just like the chariot.

One of these is called the set of the five "skandhas", or five "heaps" that give a picture of how a person quite literally "stacks up". First is "form", the body, including sense organs and the nervous system. The second is known as "feeling", or sensation. This is not "feeling" in the sense of emotion. It is rather "feeling" in the understanding of a sensory experience, that is to say: we "like", we "dislike", or it is neutral. This is pre-conscious. This way in which the mind will have a tremendously reflexive or instinctive understanding - "like", "dislike" or "neutral" – shapes many elements of our human relationships.

So, we hear the sound of a bird singing, and there is a pre-conscious awareness of "like": I "like" the bird's singing. Sensation is simply this quality "like". It is followed by "perception", the quality of recognition. We hear the bird's singing, and we say, "Aha! A bird is singing." This intensifies our sense of being a separate entity, because we perceive that the bird singing is separate from "us" who is the hearer of the sound.

This is the capacity of the conceptual mind to put things together, to conceptualize, and to recognize things by associating them with other things. We recognize a watch as being a watch because we've seen many watches, and we put it in this category. So, here is where the mind will experience that interrelationship between the general and the specific; our perceptions are conditioned by past experience.

Often they are simply inaccurate. It's neither good nor bad, nor right nor wrong, but it can increase our suffering because this mechanism can permit us to perceive and relate with things in a way that is erroneous. It's like the conceptual mind is that part which fills in the blanks. There are things that we know, and there are things that we think we know, and we fill in the blanks to make it understood to be a conceptual whole: "Oh, that's a bird singing."

Fourth is rendered in English by the expression "mental formation", "samskara". This is where "how we have perceived" then moves on to the next step of the habitual tendencies of thinking and action that we have as a result of those concepts. Here is where the karmic momentum that has built up can lead us, in a semi-conscious way, to simply continue a previously developed pattern of behavior. These patterns will determine what we might think of as one's personality style. Becoming aware of these patterns as being patterns is useful in how we relate to others in personal contexts and also in professional or social contexts. A personality style, once it is recognized as being a pattern, can become helpful as a predictor of behavior, "If I do this, then he will do that. It is consistent with the personality style".

This quality of "personality style" is quite impersonal. To say that "this person is like that", or "that person is like this" is fuzzy thinking: it is imprecise. More precisely, "there's this style of personality"; "there's that style of personality". The behavioral patterns will be more or less fixed, more or less solid, but all of them are always subject to change. So, it can be all right to not give up on someone, or to not give up on ourselves. Behavioral patterns, or personality styles, are subject to change.

They are also subject to the application of common sense. The invitation would be to respond to them with a balance of kindness, or compassion, and wisdom: it is not the "idiot compassion" of "being nice", because one doesn't have the backbone or strength of character to be able to do otherwise, but to seek to have the balance of choosing when to be patient, with the wisdom to also know when and where to draw a line.

The fifth of the five "skandhas" is "consciousness", or awareness, the ability to discern, to know, and to understand. Consciousness is "that which knows". It's the part that puts it all together and, if we're lucky, helps us to see through the patterns of ourselves and others, and helps us to be able to let go.

Step 3: Press "Pause"

We've talked about the nature of mind in terms of action and reaction. The mind can be conditioned by our past experiences. We can behave in a way which unfolds by the momentum of that past experience almost outside of our conscious awareness.

Mindfulness practice increases our ability to have that conscious awareness. We begin to see the thinking that is happening in the conceptual mind as being part of a pattern. Regularity of sitting meditation practice supports that. Gradually, one relaxes an awareness of this particular person, or that particular incident, or this particular feeling of frustration, and understands it rather as being part of a pattern. It becomes slightly more impersonal. The interchangeable quality of it is heightened in our awareness. A person grows in the recognition, "I'm feeling frustrated about this situation. It is a precise replica of that situation six months (weeks, days, hours) ago that I was also feeling frustrated about. It's a different person; it's a different time: it's the same pattern."

It has a quality of, "here we go again". That quality of "here we go again", if we're lucky, will become increasingly experienced by the mind as really boring. When the mind gets bored enough with it, it will let the pattern go. The pattern is useful only if it provides distraction. Who would have thought that boredom would be a gateway to freedom from suffering?

The conceptual mind likes being distracted and entertained. Sure this is entertainment by means of our various gadgets, but it doesn't really require gadgets. It is any kind of fuss and bother, generated by the mind, that gets in the way of our seeing that - when it comes right down to it - the fuss and bother that we're experiencing is just a mask. It's part of the way the mind is working hard to have us see and experience the self as an unchanging solid. "This is me. This is mine. This is what I want. This is the way it is."

Everything that we experience in the context of our being human is fluid and constantly subject to change. Try to make it solid when it's not, try to hold on to it when we can't, and it will just make us more and more miserable.

Things change. To the degree that we're able to trust that it really will be all right – trust in our own ability to work with the situation, in our own inherent resourcefulness and strength - to that degree we are able to grow, adapt and change with them, eventually becoming so bored with our patterns that they fall away.

Mindfulness practice helps us to learn how to trust enough to let go of the patterns that somehow got stuck, that we hold on to even though they give us pain. We both give and receive with an open hand.

I've been considered family to a Buddhist monastery for about a decade now. The monastery is about a three hour drive away from me. I still have a very clear memory of my first visit there. It was in the winter, about the time of the winter solstice. I had come to know a friend from the abbey in different situations several times before, and over quite a sustained period. This was my first time visiting my friend who was a monk there.

The abbey is located just off what's called the "Cabot Trail" in Cape Breton, Nova Scotia which, I believe, is actually considered by National Geographic to be among the most beautiful places in the world. It's tremendously beautiful, in part because there's a coming together of oceans, and mountains, and forest. For me, at least, it has a slight quality of being at the edge of the earth: not quite "beyond here there are dragons", but with the sense that one has gone beyond.

I visited my friend at this monastery in the middle of the winter, and it was a magical Canadian winter day. We'd had a lovely day together, and we had, towards the end of the day, taken a walk up the mountain which is just right at the back of the abbey. There's a lovely shrine that's halfway up - it is a cave shrine - and there's another shrine that's right at the top. We were going to visit the shrine at the top.

When we started, the snow was falling in a gentle, and elegant, and wonderful way, almost like those children's toys where you shake the glass and the snowflakes fall in a plastic model that you're holding in your hand. It was lovely, this gentle walk up the mountain in this magical atmosphere of a Canadian winter, but when we got to the top - both of us felt it -suddenly the winds changed, and what had been a lovely walk in a gentle winter's snowfall suddenly became really quite a strong and dramatic winter storm. The wind was blowing, and the snow was falling fast and hard.

Now, my friend was born, I think, part mountain goat. He knew the paths and places on that mountain very well. He could make his way down that mountain blindfolded, and it's a very good thing because, essentially, he was. All I was able to see was the space between my eye and my glasses, which functioned a little bit as a goggle. All I could see was to place my feet in the footprints my friend left behind in the snow.

It didn't take long before I had the very wonderful experience that it wasn't my foot that was going down to the earth. It's rather the earth that was rising up to meet me. I didn't hold myself up; I was being held up. The more I relaxed, the more I allowed myself to be held.

We made it down the mountain. There was a warm cup of coffee and something warm to eat, and the snow did seem to have settled, when we had the conversation: would this visiting guest unexpectedly stay overnight at the monastery, or would we decide it would be very good for her to keep the plan that was the original plan and head back home. I also have vivid memory of that conversation with the person who is now the elder monk in that monastic community and my friend. The decision was made that this visitor was coming for a first time, and we should keep the original plan. The snow seemed to be subsiding. It was probably just fine for her to head home.

So I began my way towards the national park that has this quality of being through the mountains, mountains that are right adjacent to the ocean and surrounded by forest. I have seen real wolves on that highway making my way through that forest, stopping on the highway to let the wolf and my car stare each other down.

As you've guessed, that night the snow began to return. I began to drive more and more slowly, and my hands began to tense on the steering wheel. I realized that I wasn't able to see past my headlights. It was very disconcerting to be surrounded by a wall of white and not able to see past my headlights, until I had the very similar sensation of being tremendously held and protected. It suddenly dawned on me that I don't need to see past my headlights. I never need to see past my headlights, because I take my headlights with me wherever I go.

It's the ground that rises up to meet us, and we take our headlights with us wherever we go.

The mindfulness practices help to increase our awareness. The habitual patterns of behaviour, therefore, become increasingly transparent. We see through the patterns of ourselves and other people. How we perceive other people, and how we perceive situations generally, becomes more subtle and more refined. Increasingly, we open the possibility that we don't need to react according to these well-developed habits. We don't need to be trapped by them anymore.

A habitual pattern is very familiar, so much so that we think we know where we're going. We think we can see far into our future, and there's a reassuring quality that comes from the sense that we know who we are. We know where we're headed, we know what is ours, and we know what we want. Often the harder we hold on to what we think we know, the more we chase after what it is that we think we want, the more we increase our own suffering.

So the invitation of step number three is that, as we become increasingly able, remember to "press pause". Recognise the space in-between cause and effect. There is a space in-between stimulus and response. There is a space in-between perception and a reaction to that perception. We can "press pause" in that space in-between, and feel it out, carefully choosing a next step. We don't need to see so very far into our future: we take our headlights with us wherever we go.

Chapter 3

How to Have an Emotion

"The winds don't hurt the sky."
-Adela.

Step 1: You Are Stronger Than Your Fear

You are stronger than your fear. You are stronger than your fear. If I say it again, will you hear it? You are stronger than your fear.

The mind is vast like the sky. Inherent in the sky is the sun. They are not two separate things: the sun in the sky. They are no more separate than cause and effect being separate. "Karma" is one word: "cause-effect". It is the seed and the fruit at the same time.

"The sun in the sky": it's one thing, "sun-sky". What is that "sun-sky" like? It is clear, vast, strong, flexible, open, warm, radiant, wise, intelligent and unbreakable because it is the vastness. It has no territory to defend. It is, therefore, unconquerable. One who has relaxed into this quality of the mind is "all victorious".

Sun-sky is patient. It has seen it all before. The winds may blow. The sky can work with that. The winds don't hurt the sky.

The sky is stable, and strong with a strength beyond words. It doesn't go anywhere. There is nowhere for it to go. It is the earth that moves. It spins in its rotation through days and nights. It moves in its circle the wheel of time as it goes around the sun.

We do follow the pathway of the sun. The sun doesn't go anywhere. We can know that. We can know that with a very deep knowing.

One of my favorite stories about the sun comes from Muslim tradition. It is the story of Al-Ghazali. He lived in about the year 1000 in Baghdad, during the great and glorious Muslim empire, when Western Europe fell under the shadow of the intellectual, scientific and artistic brilliance of Islam.

Al-Ghazali was a great theologian. He held the high seat at the most prestigious "madrasa", or intellectual institution, in Baghdad. He was also a great philosopher.

It bears remembering that it is Islamic tradition that will return linear, deductive logic - and the early philosophy of the ancient Greeks - to Western Europe where it had been lost. In this period, around the year 1000, great Islamic philosophers interact with great Jewish philosophers, and great Christian thinkers: they flourish and thrive together, in part, because of the rediscovery of the work of the ancient Greeks. Muslim influence - through ancient texts lost in their Greek version but accessible in Arabic translation and studied by Muslim thinkers - return ancient Greek logic to Western Europe, giving rise to the Renaissance, to Western Europe's interest in the scientific method, and to the rise of technologies that will make the explorations of the colonial period possible. We are, indeed, parts of a whole.

Al-Ghazali was a great theologian and a great philosopher, a brilliant intellect who enjoyed social prestige and what many might understand to be success. Then, one day, on the way to work, he saw a coin lying on the ground. He bent over to pick up the coin, and somehow it struck him, the idea that he would hold the coin up to the sun.

He held the coin up to the sun, and he looked at the coin: the coin covered the sun. It looked, from that perspective, that the coin was bigger than the sun. If the coin wasn't bigger than the sun, how could the coin be covering the sun? Of course, he knew the sun is bigger than the coin. In that moment, he realized: external sensory perception, the information that we gather by means of our senses – eyes, ears, nose, tongue, touch - is subject to error. There are some things that we can learn through an investigation of the outside world, but there are also things that we perceive with our senses that are simply demonstrably inaccurate.

Al-Ghazali knows the sun is bigger than the coin because he just knows. It will lead him to engage another stage of his quest.

He will leave his position in Baghdad, and he will find a Sufi, that is, a teacher in the Islamic mystical tradition. He will live simply, in this time of his life, as a spiritual seeker. Eventually, he will come to be recognised as not only Islam's greatest theologian and philosopher, but also its greatest mystic, and he will combine these three abilities in a way that has strong influence in the unfolding of Islamic history and culture.

There are some things we just know. We can trust that, even when they don't seem to make sense to the logic of our conceptual mind. The sun is always there in the "sun-sky". Even if we can't see it, it hasn't gone anywhere. There is nowhere for it to go.

You are stronger than your fear.

The understanding that the enlightened mind is our authentic, genuine nature, that it is always with us - inside us, around us, present with us in the way that space is present with us, in the way that anything is 99.999% space - is sometimes named, in Buddhist tradition, "Buddha nature".

The enlightened mind is always with us. We just need to notice that, connect to that inherent wisdom and kindness, intelligence and strength, and foster that in our experience of ourselves and our experience of others.

So the Buddhist teacher Asanga would say, for example:

"If an inexhaustible treasure were buried in the ground beneath a poor man's house, the man would not know of it, and the treasure would not speak and tell him "I am here!". Likewise a precious treasure is contained in each being's mind. This is the true state, which is free from defilement. Nothing is to be added, and nothing to be removed."

The enlightened mind is inside each of us, in the way that oxygen is inside of air, or butter is inside of milk.

It can be helpful to learn to look at clouds from the perspective of the sun. Be on the earth, look up at the sky, and some days those clouds can look mighty thick and heavy with rain. It can be useful to remember: you are stronger than your fear in the way that the sky is bigger than the clouds.

Clouds come, and they go. They are constantly changing. They are not solid. The winds don't hurt the sky.

What is an emotion? What are these clouds?

Emotions are thoughts with energy. We can learn to work with them in a way which is similar to how we work with thoughts. They come, and they go. They are not solid.

Mindfulness practitioners, who have meditated one generation after the next for thousands of years, have recorded a list of certain varieties and types of clouds, certain varieties and types of emotions, that it can be helpful to consider.

It's a bit like saying, "Yes, there are clouds in the sky. There are the cumulus clouds, the big white puffy ones. There's stratus clouds, the layer that looks like fog up against the sky, the layer of grey. There's the nimbostratus clouds, the big heavy rain clouds."

The emotions that, as humans, we tend to experience are named in a list known to Buddhist tradition as the "kleshas". The word "klesha" means literally "obscuration", that which blocks or obscures our experience of the awake or enlightened mind, in the same way that clouds can block our vision or view of the sun in the sky.

The first three "kleshas" connect very closely to those pre-conscious sensations that we talked about in relation to the second "skandha": "like", "dislike", "neutral". These three become the first in the list of the "kleshas", and there have been times in Buddhist teachings where these three were considered to be "the kleshas": sometimes it's a list of three, sometimes five, sometimes six, sometimes seven. It just depends a bit how we count it.

Passion is first of these emotions that, like a cloud, can obscure our direct awareness of the enlightened mind. What's being communicated here is not passion in the sense of a vibrant and dynamic, engaged passionate delight in being alive, a sense of joy of the kind we might experience if we were to run on the beach. This is passion in the sense of a lust, the clinging, craving quality of, "I want". I want *that*. I want that person. I want that thing, that material object. If I just had the right pair of jeans, the right kind of makeup, if only I were blonde, then I'd be happy. I want that thing out there. I want it to be mine. I want. I want. I want.

I think of it, with affection, as the golden retriever position. My beautiful Sarah-the-wonder-dog had a strong understanding of, "I want". It was characteristic in our house that there were marks on the kitchen floor in front of the cupboard with the cookie jar. She would stand looking at the cupboard with the cookie jar... saliva dripping on the floor at the very idea of the cookie jar. "I want": it's a relatively easy behavioral pattern to recognise in ourselves.... the golden retriever position... after the cookie jar. I want.

Aggression is the second of the "kleshas", the second type of cloud. It can be even easier to recognise: "don't want", "dislike", "push away". Again, the instinct is pre-cognitive. So, it isn't "I dislike"; it doesn't have the "I" quality attached to it at the early pre-cognitive stage. It's simply "dislike", "don't want", "push away".

It shows itself in anger or any kind of violence. There is a full spectrum, a range we use to express the basic gesture of "push away": "I don't want".

The third in the list of the "kleshas" can be the hardest to recognize in ourselves and others. It is "ignorance", in the literal sense of "not knowing". It can be traced to that pre-cognitive sensation we described as "neutral": "to not know", to some degree to choose not to know. It expresses itself in neglect, for example. What are those things, what are those behaviors, or those patterns, those problems in our lives that we choose to not know?

If you were to go to a large house party, or perhaps a crowded shopping mall - in a social space where there are 100 people– about eighty of the people we won't even see. Then, there will be those we "like", who look "really nice" to us, that we want to go and talk to, and there will be those we "push away". They feel a bit creepy. We'll stay away from them.

It can be hard to recognize this quality of "not knowing", so I can offer that, for me, it's experienced in the mind as confusion, a fuzziness of thinking. If my mind is feeling confusion - slightly lost, off balance, that it doesn't quite know what's going on, awkward, thick, foggy - then I know to work with it in the way that I would work with this third "klesha", "not knowing". There are ways to work with all of these.

Next on the list is jealousy. Jealousy is not always considered a discrete or independent "klesha" because it is a combination of the first two. Jealousy is a combination of lust and aggression: "I want because you have". Go into it a bit more deeply, and it can become, "I want to take it away from you because you have it".

Item five on our list is pride. Pride is the first in the list of seven Cardinal Sins in Christian tradition, and it's actually the sin ascribed to Lucifer. Yet, pride became confused with "success" in the colonial period, and, as a contemporary culture, we're still working our way out of that.

Pride is a combination of aggression and ignorance. "I will raise myself up by pushing you down." The element of ignorance is not knowing that the self is not a solid. Pride is reflected in someone who believes they are at the center of the universe. Everything in the universe ought to be revolving around them. Should someone disagree with the fact that "I" am at the center of the universe, then "I" will engage a range of acts of aggression on those people until they come to the obvious conclusion that "I", in fact, am superior: I require them to lay their power and authority at my feet. I should own all the wealth in the world. Of course, I should be controlling all the territory. I am fundamentally superior; the world revolves around me. I will destroy anyone who might dare to think otherwise.

Pride can be quite dangerous, and it can lead people to cause a great deal of harm. Neither women nor men have the copyright on pride, but there can be gendered distinctions in the way that it is expressed or communicated.

The next "klesha" is not part of the historic, classical list. It is considered a "klesha" in this time period, however, because it is a "klesha" experienced in a wide-spread, culturally common way at this time. This is the "klesha" of "doubt". It was personally very useful for me when I began to recognize doubt as being a "klesha", which is to say a variety of cloud: not solid, not real. It comes, and I can let it go.

Doubt can be a trap. It's expressed when we decide that something is fundamentally bad or fundamentally unworkable. Decide there is no solution, and that itself will be the obstacle that prevents us from engaging our resources to find a solution.

Doubt is a thinking pattern that would be something like this. There's no point in my studying for the test. Why would I bother studying for the test? I know I'm just going to fail anyway. It doesn't really matter if I fail, because I'm not going to be able to go to graduate school, anyway. I'm never going to be able to find a job, because there are no jobs to be found. I'm probably just going spend the rest of my life living in my parent's basement. So why would I bother studying for the test?

Everyone knows the environment is utterly, totally and completely collapsing. Scientists have proven that it's absolutely beyond repair, so there's no point in even trying. That means humans are on a path that is suicidal. So I should just go out, drink and be merry, because tomorrow we die. All governments are corrupt. All religious institutions are corrupt. Every marriage will end in divorce. Everything is utterly and completely hopeless. So why bother? The "trap of doubt" sounds something like that.

The proposal we're being asked to consider is that all situations are fundamentally workable. In my experience, any solution is there inside the problem, in the same way that the seed is contained inside the fruit. Often we can find a solution, if we pose the question of the problem accurately.

It seems to me that, if we can put vehicles on Mars, we do have the collective intelligence and resourcefulness as a species to handle our environmental situation, for example. It would require that, as a planet, humans cooperate and value our mutual survival more than individual self-interest.

All of the "kleshas" are variant expressions of fear. They are all rooted in fear. That root fear is an understanding we have - in some dusty, cobwebby, back corner of our awareness - that the self isn't really a solid.

The behavioral patterns associated with the "kleshas" can be exacerbated, or increased, if the identity of the one expressing this behavior is threatened or challenged. Put that person in a situation that is somehow a threat to that person's self-concept, and the "kleshas" can increasingly harden, stiffen, solidify, almost concretize, so that they become more and more of a trap for oneself and for others.

How do we work with these emotions in order that we experience them as a less and less of a trap, and gradually increase our sense of openness and relaxation with space?

Recognize the "klesha" as being like a cloud. Jealousy is just jealousy. Aggression is just aggression. It may be experienced by you, but it is not personal to you, any more than the oxygen moving in and out of your lungs is personal to you.

The feelings are not solid. Like clouds, they come, and they go. Observe them as they come and they go, and we find that they form habitual patterns, in a way very comparable to how our thoughts can form habitual patterns: an emotion is a thought that is charged with energy.

Know how to engage the "pause" button. Know how much of the energy of an emotion we can be present with, and work with, and when it's too much. Know when it's so much that we should be asking for external support: it's always useful to consider asking for external support. If, for example, I'm feeling very angry - so angry that it would not be possible for me to be in a situation without acting out that anger - then that would be a really good moment to go for a walk.

Part of working with the emotion is putting ourselves in a situation where we can be aware of, and feel the energy of the emotion, without repressing it and also without acting it out.

In the example of aggression, if yelling back at someone who is in the process of yelling at you was going to be successful, I feel it would have worked by now. This is the case with individual human conflict, with conflict as it appears in institutional settings, and in larger social contexts. From this perspective, no one wins a war. War itself is the expression of failure. It can take a strong or steady mind to be able to "press pause" in that space in-between and choose a more skillful response. Our ability to do that will increase as our meditation or mindfulness practice becomes further developed.

The mindfulness practice becomes itself a place where we can touch, or taste, the emotion enough to recognize the habitual pattern and be aware of it without acting out. Over time, the habitual pattern will become understood by the mind to be no longer be entertaining. Sometimes it feels not so much that I am letting go, but rather that I can't hold on any more. When the mind gets truly and thoroughly bored with something, it will naturally let it go in the way that our autumn leaves in Canada will naturally fall from the tree.

You are stronger than your fear.

Step 2: Apply Kindness

The emotions that we've described as the "kleshas" – lust, aggression, ignorance, jealousy, pride, doubt and fear - are not the full range of how we would describe human emotion of the type that tends to challenge us. They are the basis, however: other emotions that are challenges we experience are variations of these. All of these are expressions of fear.

In this way, to work with any emotion that is challenging us is a type of working with fear. This means that there is a medicine that can be quite widely applied. Perhaps it's a bit like peppermint essential oil or frankincense essential oil. It's one medicine that can be applied and be of benefit in many different circumstances. That medicine is kindness.

I'm so sorry you're feeling afraid.

I'm so sorry you're feeling anxious.

I'm so sorry it feels like you're shattered into pieces, that you're shivering and alone, that no one could ever see, and no one could understand, that you're cold, and you'll never be warm again.

I'm so sorry you're feeling angry. You have every right to be feeling angry.

I'm so sorry for your suffering.

I'm so sorry that you are feeling so hurt.

I'm so sorry that you're feeling betrayed. You were brave enough to trust. I'm so sorry that you were hurt because of that courage to trust. May you learn to be able to trust again.

I'm so sorry the responsibility feels so heavy. There are so many people depending on you. You carry the weight of that, the heaviness of that. I'm so sorry it's so hard.

I'm so sorry for your loss. She died. He died. Somehow it feels you could never be whole again. In some way, it's freeing to have her no longer in your life. It's so confusing. I'm just so sorry.

I'm so sorry that you feel you need dye your hair blonde, or have a body that's that much skinnier, or somehow make yourself into what you think they need you to be, in order that you could be accepted, in order that you could be heard, in order that you could be loved. It's so hard. Turn yourself into what you think they want you to be, and there's no you left anymore, and so you can't actually be accepted, and you can't actually be heard, and you can't actually be loved. I'm so sorry it feels like such a trap.

I'm so sorry that you're so lonely. You feel like no one can ever see you. No one can ever really know what you are, so that you can never actually be touched. You can't actually be loved. I'm sorry you are lonely.

I'm so sorry that you were so hurt, that you're born in a culture - you're in a situation - that feels so unsafe... where so many people were hurt so badly it's like we don't even remember what safety feels like anymore. It's so unfair. You have every right to be angry. I'm so sorry.

I'm so sorry you're feeling so guilty....that somehow, to be truly alive, you felt like you needed to disappoint so many people who wanted, who needed you, to be something other than what you are. I'm so sorry for the weight of the guilt.

I'm so sorry you were hurt when you were young, that you learned that the world was frightening, that there was no one safe to ask for help. So you learned never to ask for help. I'm so sorry for all of those parts of you that are still living in that place of fear, crawled back in the dark corners hidden in the cupboards under the stairs. They still haven't understood that it's over, and it is safe to come out now. I'm so sorry he hurt you. I'm so sorry she disappointed you. I'm so sorry they hurt you. I'm so sorry that you are dishonored, disrespected, cast aside. I'm so sorry you're feeling afraid.

Apply kindness.

It's patient. It's gentle. It's so brave. It's so strong.

And it's a homing signal.

It helps the fear to remember warm, safe, open, free. It helps the fear to remember that it's safe to let go. When it lets go, and relaxes, it's able to return to its inherent, genuine nature, in the way that the wave returns to the sea.

It's basic, inherent nature - of any mind including yours - is kind, wise and strong.

Apply medicine that helps the mind to remember that. Slowly, it will relax, and come home to itself.

One expression used to describe this is to "put the fearful mind in a cradle of a loving kindness". Held in a cradle of kindness, slowly it will relax.

If you do meditation practice where you're giving the mind a resting place which is the physical sensation of the breath, as it comes in and out of the body, that breath can sometimes feel like it is a cradle of kindness.

Life-giving, supporting, strong, holding the mind, helping it to relax: it's medicine: for fresh wounds; gaping, open, raw wounds; deep, infected wounds; old wounds that fester under the surface; and it can even heal scars.

Kindness, in this way, is something that we offer ourselves. When it is understood like that, it would be expressed in Sanskrit by the term "maitri". It's a quality of being brave enough to accompany ourselves in the journey that is the course of our lives.

Can we be present with ourselves? Can we bear witness to ourselves? Can we be willing to hear and know ourselves? Can we receive ourselves with this balance of gentleness, wisdom, strength, insight, knowing ourselves enough that we can receive ourselves as we are. Can we experience ourselves in any moment as we are? Receiving ourselves, welcoming ourselves is a way of helping ourselves to come home to this genuine nature.

That genuine nature is outside of the constraints or limitation of the conceptual mind. This is to say, it is outside of the constraints or limitations that we might impose upon ourselves, in the variety of ways that we might think we ought to be - in this, or that, or some other way - better than what we are.

Be gentle enough with ourselves, be kind enough with ourselves: gradually, the mind can relax its hold on the boundaries or limitations of the concepts we impose on ourselves ... enough to be able to see that everything we wish for we already are.

You are enough. Absence of absence. Brilliant, warm, rich, resourceful, intelligent: able to shine as bright as the sun-sky. Vast, flexible and unconquerable, because there is no territory to defend.

Kindness is called the antidote to aggression. The energy that is fear cannot be sustained in the presence of kindness.

It can only relax. The more we help the fear to feel safe enough to receive kindness, the more we guide it to a place where it can only let go and relax.

Being present with ourselves in this way helps us to increase our capacity to offer kindness with this gentle mix of insight, wisdom and strength, to be present with others in the course of their journey. This is known by the Sanskrit word "karuna", compassion. Compassion is the ability to be present with and feel someone else's suffering at least as vividly as one would feel one's own. It is a tremendous expression of strength, when one has sufficiently ripened in relation to one's own experience to be able to hold a steady mind, a strong back, and an open heart in relation to others.

That is traditionally what is being taught through the mindfulness practices, and, in particular, through the style of meditation practice known as "calm abiding", or shamatha. It is reflected the physical posture associated with that practice, sometimes called "mountain pose". There is a strong back. There is an interdependent relationship between that strong back and the strength of the open heart. These two create a seat in which to foster the fearlessness of the stable mind, strong because it is sufficiently relaxed to be flexible enough to be where we are when we're there. Kindness and compassion are among the greatest possible human expressions of genuine strength, bearing witness to these inherent qualities of mind itself.

There is no difference between self and other when understood in this context. What we give to others, we also receive. The theory of karma reflects this. There is a relationship between cause and effect: how I think, or speak, or act in relation to the outside world can only be reflected back to me. It's the boomerang effect.

This includes thoughts, words or actions that bring benefit. Since there is, ultimately, no difference between self and other, the kindness I communicate in the world also, in some way, comes back to me.

It's a subtle and organic expression of reciprocity. If the atmosphere that we move in is infused with kindness, in some way, we will also swim in those waters.

Kindness here is distinct, as we have seen, from what contemporary Buddhist slang calls "idiot compassion". Idiot compassion is kindness in the absence of wisdom: confused kindness; kindness without discernment; kindness that does "not know". This is that quality of "being nice" because we don't know how to do otherwise: we don't know how to communicate a boundary, or to command respect, or to say "no"; we don't want to "cause harm", in the sense of not wanting to ruffle any feathers. It can be an intermediate stage on the way to an expression of "maitri" or "karuna".

What "maitri" or "karuna", this quality of kindness, is seeking to accomplish is the balance of kindness and wisdom simultaneously. It is interested in exploring the strength of being able to do what is genuinely and honestly kind, to the best of our ability, with our compassionate discernment and insight. This means doing what will be honestly helpful, even if it is hard, socially uncomfortable, or not what would be socially expected. Sometimes this is described as an ability to be "gentle but tough".

Wisdom in the absence of compassion can also be an intermediate step on the journey. Sometimes it's a very important intermediate step to have the wisdom not to confuse aggression with strength.

If a person is being bullied, or in some other way abused, it can be useful to have an insight that sounds something like, "I am so sorry for you that you are such a coward that you need to try and push yourself up by pushing other people down. I am so sorry for you that you are *such* an *idiot*."

To not confuse aggression with strength can help to set a person free from a situation which is, in some way, unsafe. It can be a way of reclaiming one's own voice and one's own authority. It is an expression of wisdom in the absence of compassion. We may not be ready yet to balance wisdom with the compassion that can only come from the safety of distance.

A situation like that is a kind of trap for everyone involved. We may be able, over time, to develop compassion for that person's suffering as part of our process of learning how to let go. Our letting it all go, when the time is right, can help to set us free. This is also a kind of wisdom with compassion for ourselves: knowing what to accept and what to reject.

Step 3: Give It Space

Sometimes we push away emotions that we don't like, that might frighten us because they are strong and feel overwhelming, or emotions that for some other reason feel uncomfortable. We don't want to feel scared. We don't want to feel lonely. We don't want to feel angry, so we can push these things away.

In some sense, it is an expression of this pre-conscious instinct we've talked about: "like", "push away", "ignore". If we push away an emotion that we don't like, and build up a wall against it, it is possible it can build to a point where it feels so big it might crush us. If we push away from an emotion that we don't like by trying to run away from it, we can set up a pattern where it can feel like that emotion is chasing us. By seeking to distract ourselves – drugs, alcohol, sex, entertaining gadgets – we may try to ignore it, but squishing it down like that can just make us feel like we are sinking.

This can grow even stronger if we have the impression that we're supposed to feel happy all of the time. "If I'm not feeling happy all of the time, there must be something wrong." I may not have the skills to be able to work with what I'm feeling, so I might push away, or run away, or otherwise try to mask or hide.

It would be like asking the earth to stop rotating so that it's always sunshine and daylight, and we never cycle through the rhythms between darkness and light which are a natural part of our process.

It's like asking the sky to never have clouds. Somehow we're afraid of the storms. We'll try to mask and hide so that we try to create a shelter from the wind, but somehow that shelter from the wind only makes the wind blow harder. It blows hard against the resistance of our walls instead of just blowing through us like through the screen of a door.

Part of what happens as a gradual result of meditation practice is that the mind develops confidence in its own strength and ability to work with its own experience, and be present with things, be present with feelings, or even be present with people *as they are*, without needing or wishing that the circumstance somehow be different. We increase in our ability – gently, patiently - to be able to taste all of our feelings, to be willing to live all of our experience, and appreciate, even, that all of this is somehow part of being alive.

In eastern Canada, where I am at the moment, there are four distinct seasons in the year. The cycle does move, in clearly visible ways, from spring, to summer, to autumn, to winter, to spring again. Each of these seasons can have something I might experience as suffering. It's too hot; it's too cold; it's too windy, too damp, too cloudy; it's too foggy. Something's not right; something's not enough.

Those exact seasons can also have elements that I might appreciate. There are the first flowers of the year coming up in the garden. Now it is strawberry season. Now it is warm enough to go swimming in the sea.

Perhaps I'll go for a walk and enjoy the colours of the autumn trees, or the gentle falling of a winter's snow by moonlight.

From this perspective, the situation itself is neither good nor bad. It is a question of how I am relating to or working with this situation in any particular moment. Do I push away what I don't want and build a resistance? Am I able to look inside that situation and find a way to enjoy that? Am I going to be in the situation somehow ignoring it altogether, so caught up in my own internal world that I hardly even know that the outside world is changing from one season to the next?

Can we feel all of our feelings, knowing that feelings, like the seasons, will come and they go? The nature of the sky is vast and warm, like the sun, but the sky also has clouds. I have thoughts and feelings - some I will like, some I will dislike, some I will ignore - but all of it is part of my experience of a human life.

Being able to be present with all of it helps me, in some way, to be more alive.

Learning how to feel all of our feelings is a gradual process and a set of skills that can be developed over time. Among those skills is an ability to be able to feel it and also give it space. It is an example of the way that space, the space in-between, enlivens us. Know if you need help in order to work with some emotions, and know that it's always okay to ask for help and to engage your resourcefulness to be able to find the help that you need.

There is a traditional way of giving an emotion space that may be helpful as part of this larger journey. It is called working with "shenpa". A Buddhist nun named Pema Chodron has taught this ancient teaching in our contemporary time. Her work is available in many places; you may wish to look online for examples of how she teaches "working with 'shenpa'".

We have described emotion as being a thought...with energy. Sometimes that thought with energy can leave us in a bit of a tizzy, and set our heads spinning, so to speak.

Usually, we experience this as some kind of narrative, some kind of story that spins around in our head. We can find ourselves wanting to communicate that storyline with others telling them, over and over, about this horrible situation, those horrible people, this horrible thing that happened. As we share it, and they reinforce our story, it can feel more and more solid. Often there's a corresponding physical sensation in the body: perhaps the neck tightens, the shoulder tightens, the jaw tightens. Quite common is a feeling of tightness as if there were a circle or a band around the head at the area of the forehead or temples. It turns in a spin; it has a tornado quality to it.

The more we tell the story to ourselves and others, the more the energy builds. The more the energy builds, the more we tell the story to ourselves and others. It will often have a sensation of heat or indignation we can hear in the voice, "I can't believe that he did that! He did that again! Can you believe he did that again? He did that horrible thing. I will never forgive him. If he does that one more time, let me tell you...". It can sound something like that.

Notice: the energy is building the more the story is told, and the story is intensifying as the energy is building. It is an interdependent relationship.

The emotion exists because of the thought. The thought exists because of the emotion.

The emotion can be an expression of lust, aggression, ignorance, jealousy, pride, doubt or fear. The mechanism is consistent and will express itself in a similar way, regardless of the content of the emotion, and regardless of the content of the story that we are telling ourselves. The more it goes, the more solid the whole thing can become. It becomes medicine, therefore, to give it space and help it become more fluid again.

We start with the possible. We start with the small stuff.

Find a story that is spinning around in your hand about something that is relatively small, some behavior - out there somewhere - that's irritating you. Maybe he didn't do the dishes – again - and you're feeling frustrated about that.

When I first learned how to do this practice, I would do it curled up in bed, with my head under the covers. Later I graduated to doing it in a hot bath. It can be helpful to learn this practice in an environment where you are feeling as safe and protected as possible.

Then begin by placing the mind in an atmosphere of kindness. This is the first step in how to "give it space". I'm so sorry you're feeling so frustrated. I'm so sorry you're so angry.

Sometimes, for me, that's enough right there. If I give it space by giving myself permission to feel the feeling, sometimes the internal dialogue will sound like this, "It's okay to be angry. You can be angry if you want to"...and I'll hear a response in a distant corner of my mind, "but I don't want to be angry". "OK, you don't have to be angry if you don't want to". Sometimes, just that small amount of space - permission to be who and what I am, and to feel whatever it is I'm feeling in that moment - is itself enough to help me let go.

The formal practice of working with "shenpa" begins with giving ourselves space in a very safe environment. Can we give ourselves a first gesture of kindness? "I'm so sorry you're feeling so frustrated". That can help to relax it enough to be able to work with it.

Then, allow the mind to become aware of the story. He didn't do the dishes, again! Having become aware of the story, let go! Just let go of the story. Drop it.

What we're doing is separating the emotion from the thought. They exist in an interdependent relationship. The one cannot be sustained in the absence of the other. So, just let go of the story. We're left with the sensation of the emotion: frustration.

Then, let me feel the frustration as directly, and utterly, and fully, and completely as absolutely possible. Feel the emotion directly - without the story that holds it up: it will dissipate and relax within 90 seconds.

It's like what we were saying about fear if placed in an atmosphere of kindness. Fear just can't be sustained in an atmosphere of kindness. It will relax into its own nature, in this case, when it's not being propped up by the concepts that put us in a spin.

The thoughts and the emotions - as we have seen - can appear in our lives and in our awareness in a pattern that's quite habitual. It's possible that the sensation of frustration - in relation to something like the dishes - may return.

If this happens, repeat steps one through three. Begin by placing oneself in an atmosphere of kindness. Then, when we're ready, let go of the story. Taste the emotion as directly, and fully, and utterly as possible. It will dissipate within 90 seconds.

As our awareness of the habitual pattern and process gradually increases, we will notice faster and faster the triggers that might set off the cycle of a habitual thought or habitual emotion. Over time, we learn how to resist the temptation - as Pema Chodron quite famously said - to bite the hook.

Why does this work?

Our list of emotions – lust, aggression, ignorance, jealousy, pride, doubt, fear: we said they were like clouds in the sky. We said that clouds aren't the basic fundamental nature of the sky, but rather they appear. They appear to be real, and solid sometimes, when in fact they're not. It's this distinction between appearance and reality which goes back in Indian tradition to very ancient times.

Tibetan Buddhist tradition will develop, in particular, the understanding that these emotions – lust, aggression, ignorance, jealousy, pride, doubt, fear - are all part of our process of growing up into spiritual maturity, as the human ripens, or progresses along the path. Each of these emotions, in some sense, is a gateway. Each is part of the organic process of how the mind awakens to its enlightened qualities. We gradually grow from the "confused expression" to the "awake expression" of each of these qualities.

Tibetan Buddhist tradition is a wisdom tradition from a culture of people who lived in the planet's highest mountain range, in a time long before Netflix. They had a well-developed practice of people meditating in caves for long periods of time, often for decades. The tradition was communicated through the generations in a series of master-student relationships. Through the practice of meditation, this culture sought to examine and understand the internal world of the human experience. This is comparable, and also in contrast, to the Western European interest in the external natural sciences that would lead to its focus on matter or technology. Buddhist tradition is a science of mind.

The observation made by this oral tradition is that the experience of lust, aggression, ignorance, jealousy, pride, doubt or fear is part of an organic process of the mind waking up to its enlightened state. It is not personal; it's impersonal in the way that gravity or oxygen is not personal. From this perspective, aggression is just aggression; jealousy is just jealousy. That person's jealousy, my jealousy, the other person's jealousy: in my working with it, I don't need to take any of these things personally. Jealousy is just jealousy; pride is just pride.

I don't need to see pride in a way that will solidify a difference between self and other. "That person's" pride that drives me around the bend: it doesn't belong to that person in any personal way, any more than the oxygen in my lungs belongs to me, or the water in my body belongs to me. We've shared these with the dinosaurs. If we are fortunate, it will be shared by many for thousands of years to come.

According to the tradition, lust or passion is simply the confused expression of compassion, or "karuna" as we have described it.

Aggression is simply the confused expression of the precise same energy which in its awakened state will manifest as kindness ("maitri"). That's why we observed kindness is the antidote to aggression, that aggression cannot be sustained in an environment or atmosphere of kindness. Kindness is the awake expression of the exact same energy that is aggression. It is almost like the kindness that's inside the aggression knows that. Give it the homing signal, allow it to have some way to remember its own state, and it will relax.

Again, if one chooses to experiment, it's good to begin small and start with the possible. Maybe there is a roommate, or a work colleague, who's experiencing frustration, a form of aggression, the instinctive response to "push away". Hear their story with an atmosphere of kindness and experiment to see how long it will be before that frustration relaxes. It can be powerful enough that one person who holds a stable mind, and an open heart, and an atmosphere of kindness can be enough to make a difference even in a room full of angry people.

The tradition holds that ignorance - this quality of neglect, "not knowing", or choosing not to know, the confusion itself - is the *unawakened* expression of the exact same energy which, in its awakened or enlightened state, will express itself as wisdom.

The energy or emotion of jealousy is just the confused version of the exact same energy which - in its awakened expression - is equanimity: that very balanced, stable state of mind able to be present with a range of emotions without being too much fussed and bothered by any of them.

The "klesha", or confusion, of pride is the exact same energy which - in its awakened state - will express itself as humility. There is no way to become more humble than by working with one's pride. Pride is based in fear; it is an expression of weakness: humility is the corresponding expression of strength. The relationship between these is part of the reason why pride has the instinct to want to humiliate. It's just humility backwards.

The "klesha" or confusion of doubt - when transmuted or transformed into its awakened state - will make itself known as "doubtlessness". This English language word is being experimented, or invented, to try and communicate a quality of deep confidence. It is confidence in the basic nature, the basic decency, the basic workability of things. It is deep and inherent trust, that deep knowing, like Al-Ghazali's knowing that the sun is bigger than the coin. It is a confidence which underlies, pervades and is stronger than the ideas we might hold onto with the conceptual mind.

And fear. The energy that we experience as fear - when transmuted or transformed into its awake expression - will be "fearlessness". This deep courage is able to be present with the full expression of our experience as persons.

The tradition would hold that there is no way to become more kind unless we are willing – in measured and appropriate ways - to taste our aggression: not repressing it, and not acting out. There is no way to become more wise unless we are willing to work with our confusion.

The experience of the "kleshas", these confused aspects of the mind, are therefore somewhat like the unfolding of the pedals of a rose as it begins its organic process of opening. It will unfold one petal at a time as the mind continues its journey of ripening, letting go, and opening, relaxing into its inherent nature: kind, wise and strong.

Chapter 4

How to Cope With Hard Things

*"The strength of our character
is carved by our wounds."*
- Adela.

Step 1: Look in the Mirror

This is something I learned from personal experience. It has the quality of being well earned and hard won. I offer it in case it may be of benefit to you.

We have just described the interrelationship between some confused emotions and their enlightened expression. We considered the possibility that aggression is kindness backwards, or that lust is compassion backwards.

In my experience, our mind has the ability to show us what it is that we most need to see. Sometimes it happens through the direct or enlightened expression, by offering us a situation where we might be experiencing kindness, for example.

Sometimes it happens by showing us what it is we need to see in a mirror, which is to say the mirror image of the thing. In this relationship between appearance and reality, appearance can be just reality backwards.

So, for example, if there is a dialogue or story that is persisting in my mind - a story that might be there when I go to sleep, and there again when I wake up - enough that it is annoying, and beginning to get boring, it can be useful to pay careful attention to what is being communicated in the content of that story.

We've talked about "shenpa", and how just letting go or dropping a storyline can release us, or set us free from, an emotion that has us somewhat entrapped. In my experience, however, the storyline often does have wisdom and insight inside of it...if I'm able to "flip it" and see what it is trying to tell me by holding up a mirror.

Let's imagine an internal dialogue that sounds something like this, "He's trying to take authority and control territory that does not belong to him". Particularly if it is an internal dialogue that persists, and has a healthy dose of frustration attached to it, it can be useful to explore what happens if I just reverse subject and object.

My mind is seeing it in a mirror.

What I'm seeing is "he" who is trying to steal authority and control a territory that does not belong to him. What if my mind is showing me what I need to see backwards? I take the exact storyline and where there is the word "he", I replace it with the word "me".

Am I not owning my own authority? Am I not claiming ownership of the territory that is mine, that does belong to me, that is rightfully part of my own life? Can I see if there is something that I need to address in my own life that somehow relates to authority and territory? In my experience, if I can name that, and do whatever I need to do to somehow set that right, then the intensity of the external situation will often naturally, organically dissipate.

Let's try another example. "Why can't she just let go of the past? Doesn't she know that the world hasn't been like that for at least 50 years? And as much as she might want to make the world be the way it was even 10 or 15 years ago, it's just not like that anymore? So why can't she just let go of the past? She's hurting so many people by trying to make things be the way they were, and they're not!".

Do you hear the quality, or tone of indignation in the voice, a voice that says, "I know how things should be!"? So I, at least in the internal dialogue, am going to tell that person what that person needs to do?

This is a gateway to freedom from suffering. It can reverse a situation where a person is driving you around the bend to create a situation where this person can become one of the most precious teachers you may ever have.

Take the internal dialogue: reverse subject and object. Where there is the word "she", replace it with the word "me". What part of me is not letting go of the past and able to fully live in the present? What part of me wants things to be the way they were 50 years ago, or even 10 or 15 years ago, or in some past time? What part of me is struggling to adapt to a change in the present, and how am I hurting myself in this process?

What do I need to do to somehow make peace with the fact that the world isn't the way it once was and that my place in the world somehow isn't what it once was? What do I need to do to allow myself to let go of the past, in order to be able flexible enough to be more fully comfortable with the way things are now?

Figure that out, apply and do the necessary, and it is entirely possible that I won't need to look into a mirror like that anymore, and the external situation will naturally and organically dissipate all by itself...when I have dropped my end of that stick.

I have found that it would not be in my awareness - particularly if it is in my awareness in a sharp, recurring, persistent way - unless it was trying to show me something that I need to be able to see. Often appearance is just reality backwards.

This is useful in personal situations. It can also be useful in institutional or leadership situations. It can be a tremendously accurate predictor of behavior.

For example, you are being accused of trying to bring corruption into the system by unduly influencing people and bringing people onto a conversation who have no business being there. You know that it's untrue. There may be an internal dialogue that simply is seeking to refute it, or to convince yourself to be patient and wait it out.

Experiment instead with reversing subject and object. It may be that it is a precisely accurate mirror image of reality. So "flip it": she's really telling you that she is seeking to bring corruption into the system. She's telling you that she is unduly influencing people, and manipulating and pulling strings behind the scenes, to include people in the conversation who have no business being there.

Listen to the rhetoric of what you are being accused of, particularly if it is in a heightened or persistent way. "Flip it", and then follow the lines. It is quite possible that she's telling you exactly what it is that she is in the process of doing. She's telling you that by accusing you of doing it. She is communicating the reality, but the reality that she is seeing is a projection: it's reality backwards. So check out what happens if you "flip it".

There are also other situations where it can be extremely useful to have a precise and accurate predictor of behaviour. One such example is an abusive situation that is personal or otherwise.

For the sake of this example, let's assume the person behaving in an abusive way is male, and the person receiving that abuse is female. This is, of course, *not* always the case, but for the sake of a pronoun we'll imagine that to be the case in this example.

Listen carefully to the content and rhetoric of things he is accusing you of, things he is telling you that you are doing. You know that it's not true. You may have the instinct to simply deny the accusation and engage the argument. So you might say to him, "No, of course I'm not trying to steal money from you!".

Pay attention to what he is accusing you of: experiment with "flipping" the statement. Look to see if there is truth in the statement, and it is simply backwards. He is telling you that he is trying to steal money from *you*. He's telling the truth. It's simply that he's experiencing it as a projection. Therefore, he's communicating it backwards, but it is a *precise* mirror image. It is precisely backwards.

So, follow the lines. Explore the possibility that he is stealing money from you. Check it out to see if it is possible this is correct. Do what you need to do in order to be safe.

Often the appearance of a thing is just reality backwards. "Flip it", then follow the lines: check it out. There is wisdom inside the confusion and truth inside the lie.

This is something I learned by personal experience, by observing the patterns and relationships that I was seeing between what was showing up in my external world, and what was showing up in my internal world.

It's my experience that, if there is something in my external world that I feel needs to be addressed, to ask the external world to change is possible but somewhat complicated. Often it's easier to look into my internal world, and feel out what is the end of that stick that I'm holding onto. If I can figure out what I need to do to drop and let go of my end of the stick, most often the other end of the stick must also fall, and that situation in the external world will naturally dissolve.

It is similar to what Taoists call "actionless action" ("wu wei"). Can we accomplish the activity as a result of our "being", as opposed our "doing"?

This technique is not something that I have found in the teachings of Buddhist psychology. It was so consistently successful for me, however, that it allowed me to see something freshly in ancient Indian cosmology. I was able to hear a story that is told there in a new way.

Ancient Indian tradition is deeply interested in the relationship between appearance and reality. The interdependent relationship between the two is illustrated, for example, in middle Vedic literature in a story told in the Shatapatha-Brahmana.

"The gods and the demons were both born from Prajapati, lord of all creatures. They both wished to possess the inheritance of their father Prajapati, which consisted of speech: both truth and falsehood. Both of them spoke the truth, and both of them spoke falsehood, and, as they spoke alike, they were alike.

The gods then gave up falsehood and kept truth. The demons gave up truth and kept falsehood.

Then the truth which had been in the demons saw this and said, "The gods have given up falsehood and continued to keep truth. Very well, I will go there", and it went to the gods. Falsehood, which had been in the gods, saw this and said, "The demons have given up truth and continued to keep falsehood. Very well, I will go there.", and it went to the demons. The gods then spoke only truth, and the demons spoke only falsehood.

The gods, speaking truth steadfastly, became weaker and poorer, and therefore whoever speaks truth steadfastly becomes weaker and poor, but - in the end - he overcomes, as the gods overcame in the end. Then the demons, speaking falsehood steadfastly, grew strong and rich like salt soil. Therefore, one who speaks falsehood steadfastly grows strong and rich as salt soil, but - in the end - he is overcome, for in the end the demons were overcome."

What we see in the mirror is a projection. It is either our own projection, or the projection of the other person, but it is a precise projection.

There is truth inside the appearance. The appearance is false.

Can we discern the difference between appearance and reality, between the true and the false, even when truth is hidden inside the appearance, and falsehood is hidden inside of the truth?

It is one of the traditional descriptors of enlightenment: the wise can distinguish between the true and the false.

The central story of the Rig-Veda Samhita, the earliest text of the Indian subcontinent (1500 BCE) is the story of the great hero, the great warrior god Indra, and his combat with the demon of Vritra.

The story is not normally interpreted in the way I am about to tell it. I do believe that it is there inside the story, for those who have eyes to see...

From the Rig-Veda, Book 1, hymn 32:

"Now let me sing of the heroic deeds of Indra!... He killed the demon, and pierced an opening for the waters; he split open the bellies of the mountains.

He killed the [demon] who lay upon the mountain.... [and] the flowing waters rushed down to the sea.

Wildly excited like a bull, he took the "soma" [drink] for himself, and he drank from the three bowls.... Indra the Generous seized his thunderbolt to hurl it as a weapon; he killed the first born of the dragons.

Indra, when you killed the first born of dragons and overcame by your own magic the magic of the magicians, at that very moment you brought forth the sun, the sky, the dawn. Since then you have found no enemy to conquer you."

The story of the great god Indra is generally understood in terms of external combat. Indra, magnificent in size and power- and most anthropomorphic, most human-like, of the deities in the Vedic pantheon - is a great warrior....but what is his great act of heroism?

Once, in the time before time, there was a demon whose name was Vritra. His name means literally "Obstacle". This obstacle, personified as the demon Vritra, had enclosed the light and the waters inside of himself.

Indra took his weapon, the thunderbolt, which is known in Sanskrit by the word "vajra". He pierced the demon, cutting him through and setting the waters free.

In some versions of the story, it is a mountain that existed in the time before time. Sometimes, it is said the demon lay on top of this mountain.

The mountain, a primordial mountain, enclosed everything. There was no space, no water, no light. Then the great warrior Indra, strengthened having drunk the offering substance known as "soma", took his "vajra", his thunderbolt, and divided the mountain. The top became the sky; the bottom became the earth: the space in-between became the atmospheric realm in which we all live.

Indra set the sun in the sky, and he set the waters free to flow. There was life, and light, and abundance, and vigor, and vitality when Indra cut through, removed the obstacles, and allowed the waters to flow freely.

Sometimes, it is said, he set the worlds apart - the heavens and the earth - like two wheels that are separated and also connected by an axle, and that - if the worlds were unsteady - they would creak like a chariot wheel.

Most commonly, the worlds are said to be propped apart. Indra divides the mountain, sets the sun in the sky, and the heavens and earth are then propped apart by the sun.

It's not the rays of the sun that hold the earth and sun apart, like eyelids held open by toothpicks. The prop is actually the cyclical flow of the pathway of the sun as it moves across the sky, through the space in-between heaven and earth. The sun comes up, the sun comes down, the sun comes up again.

There is continuity and discontinuity simultaneously. What will give us our death is also what gives us our life. We follow the pathway of the sun.

The flow of those waters that happens, when the obstacle is removed, is what gives us the juiciness, the "aliveness". This same sap that will enliven the cosmos - flowing between heavens and the earth, in the same way that sap will flow in a tree from roots to the leaves - is the same juiciness, lifeforce, and life principle that moves inside the individual human, as the vigor, vitality, delight, humor, intelligence, creativity, strength, happiness and abundance.

How do we connect with the vigor and vitality, creative abundance, and delight? It is what's waiting for us, Indra shows us, when we cut through our obstacles.

So how does Indra cut through his? He is strengthened by "soma", and he wields his weapon which is the thunderbolt or "vajra".

What does it mean he is strengthened by "soma"? He connects with the deep strength of the mind that we discover when we connect with the "bigness" inside of our "smallness".

"Soma" is one of the precious substances that are given in offering at the ancient Indian fire offering, the ritual that connects humans, ancestors and gods. Foodstuffs are placed on the fire in order that they may be carried by the smoke as an offering to the gods.

Anything that is offered in this ritual offering symbolises the offering of the self. The way in which we as humans participate in this flow of the life principle between heaven and earth is through the offering of the self. Our strength comes from connecting by giving of ourselves: open hand, strong back, open heart.

The altar used in the Vedic fire ritual is made of five layers of brick separated by four layers of mortar, or cement; a fifth layer of mortar is on top of it all. The mortar, the cement between the bricks, is symbolically understood to be aspects of Prajapati's mortal body: hair, skin, flesh, bones and marrow. The layers of the bricks symbolically represent Prajapati's immortal body: spirit, speech, breath, eye, ear. So, in building the fire altar used for the offering, one layers the mortal and immortal aspects thus making it all immortal.

Essentially, that is what we are doing everything time we give, every time we offer with open heart and open hand: we connect our mortal aspects with our immortal aspects. We "get over" the perception of our limits and somehow touch that part of ourselves that is infinite. We touch into the deep continuity that gives us life. We are, after all, descended from Manu: only humans can give and be that which is given. In giving, we connect our immortal aspects with our mortal ones. In the centre of the first layer of the altar is placed a golden statue that symbolically represents the human: the ritual offering is the offering of the self.

The symbolism will continue, as the tradition evolves, in the ritual of the construction of the Hindu temple. The basic unit of measurement for the temple will be the body - the measurement of the human body of the patron - who is sponsoring or paying for the construction of the temple. Through his patronage, he builds a "second body" which he offers so that it may become the seat of the god.

We are strengthened by touching in with that bigness inside of our smallness. It helps us to see the difference between appearance and reality clearly. It gives us strength.

What is this "obstacle" that Indra overcomes? Our smallness. The appearance of "me" that I might try to make solid. We know the parts of us that are fake and the parts of us that are real: choose the real.

Indra's weapon is the "vajra", or thunderbolt. It is able to cut through the space in-between: heaven and earth, mortal and immortal, primordial and created worlds, appearance and reality. This word "vajra" will give its name to Vajrayana Buddhism, the aspect of Buddhist tradition most commonly associated with Tibet. Within that tradition is a Bodhisattva, a realized spiritual being, whose name is Manjushri. Bodhisattva of wisdom, he wields a sword in the way that Indra wields his "vajra".

The sword that is wisdom is the discernment to see clearly through that space in-between. This is how we overcome obstacles. This is how we cut through: can we distinguish between the true and the false?

Is there a difference between the gods and the demons, between appearance and reality? What is actually going on in the relationship between Indra and the demon Vritra, between the hero and how he is working to overcome the "obstacle"?

We hear it in Rig-Veda 1.32.4:

"Indra, when you killed the first born of dragons and overcame by your own magic the magic of the magicians, at that very moment you brought forth the sun, the sky, the dawn. Since then, there is no enemy to conquer you."

The terms here being rendered as "magic" and "magician" are Sanskrit words that we have seen: "maya" and "mayin", one who possesses "maya". Both Hindu and Buddhist traditions will use the word "maya" to name the appearance that we cut through in order to become enlightened.

The word "mayin", however – one who possesses the ability to move in this space in-between the appearance of things that is both real and somehow not – is applied in the Rig-Veda to humans, and demons, and gods. On 37% of occasions, the word "mayin" is applied to demons. Typically, it is "Vritra". The gods also are possessors of "maya", and Indra is said to be most gifted in "maya".

In the fight between them, Vritra - the enemy - is shown to be a mirror of the god. These old visionary poets tell us again and again that the enemy is attacked with his own weapons. The god bends with his own strength the strength of his rival. By your speech cross the speech of the enemy. Fortress should attack a fortress. The enemy is the one who practices the magic we practice against him. Indra, by his own magic, overcomes the magic of the magicians.

God and demon, true and false: the one mirrors the other. Look closely enough in that mirror, and we will see there is no difference. This applies to the many demons we encounter in the course of our days.

The god versus demon story told in the story of "Indra versus Vritra" will become the prototype for all of Hinduism's subsequent god versus demon stories. There are many of them. A most famous example would be the story of Rama versus Ravana in the epic poem of the classical period known as the "Ramayana".

Good guys versus bad guys, cops against robbers, super heroes against super villains: every culture in my awareness is replete with god versus demon stories. Is it that the ancestors of Indo-European tradition brought these stories into the seed cultures of many lands? Certainly. There is, however, more.

Indra's story is showing us the combined strength of two very basic aspects of the human mind. We have the ability for strength, the greatness of calm stability that we touch in with by means of connection, by means of generosity. That deep strength of the mind is the stability and deep peace trained by "calm abiding" practice, or "shamatha". The second principle aspect of the mind Indra is showing us is awareness: insight, wisdom, discernment, the ability to distinguish appearance and reality trained by the mindfulness practice known as "vipashyana".

We wield the sword of discernment. We create demons, and fight them, all the time. We make our own demons, just as surely as we shape our worlds by our stories.

Our minds create a sharp experience of the dualism – "this" versus "that" - to teach us to see the space in-between. It is another part of the organic process of how we wake ourselves up. We need these strengths of stability of mind – "calm abiding" – and "awareness" to be able to do it.

What is the god versus demon story that you are telling yourself at the moment?

It applies both at the level of the individual and at the level of the broader social collective: "those horrible people out there need to be destroyed by the savior, the hero me". A variation of the story would be: "those horrible people out there are trying to destroy me". In the end, the gods overcame…there were chapters in-between….

Consider the god versus demon story you are telling yourself. Notice who you are casting in the starring roles.

If they are general, blanket concepts which have energy – likely strong energy – attached to them, but which are lacking the precision of specifics, that is a sign that you are "confusing the general and the specific". You are looking through your visor.

I work at a university. In that context, the general concept "boss" is called "the administration". You can fill in your own blank. "Supervisor", "Wife", "Teacher", "Boyfriend", "Boss": it doesn't really matter. If a general concept, like "the boss", plays a starring role in the myth or story that you are telling yourself, check to see if you can tell yourself the same story using what is the one specific name of the one person involved.

If yes, this may be an indicator that you are perceiving correctly, that there really is something "out there" that needs your attention. Especially if it is a safety issue of some kind, please consider finding any help that you may need to support you in your situation. If you are feeling fear in any way, please trust this intelligence and find appropriate responses. Fears tells you that something *is* wrong.

Often, you can't tell yourself the same story using the one specific name of the one person involved. The mind has filtered out the specific information in order to attach itself to the general concept - "boss" - probably because some part of its self-concept or personal identity has been threatened.

This is even more likely to be the case if the mind reaches for generalised things in the past: "they are doing it again". Often both the "they" and the "it" are simply constructed concepts that don't really exist.

This is even more true if the mind is reaching to a concept of an older, "perfect" past. "Before, everything was paradise. The demon came. We conquered. Now, they are doing it again. I must conquer the demon."

God versus demon: there is no difference. What you are accusing the other person of doing, most likely, in some way, you yourself are doing....to yourself or to someone else.

Telling these stories is part of how we wake ourselves up.

See through them: what is the mirror really trying to help us to see? See that, apply it, and do the necessary, and you will have overcome this expression of confusion in the mind: one more petal open in our lotus flower coming into bloom.

Perhaps the most common metaphor for the enlightened mind is the lotus flower. The lotus flower is a water flower, like the water lily. It grows because its feet are rooted in the mud, and the murky, fuzzy, cloudy, muddy kind of water that my dog so much liked to drink. The lotus flower grows up out of that, shoots for the sky, and petal by petal it gradually opens. The result is breath-taking.

In the battle of god versus demon, often the enemy really is "us".

It is, therefore, a battle we cannot lose.

If I want to turn myself into a super hero, and "him" into a super demon, and escalate in my internal dialogue the great, horrible, most dreadful thing that "he" is doing that causes "me" to need to conquer "him", that is great.

I can go ahead and build that wall just as big and high as I want to. That will make it even more painful when I bang my head into it, as I will surely do. "He" is just a projection of "me". Perhaps "he" is projecting onto "me". I would not be in the story, if I were not holding my end of that stick.

I can bang up against that wall just as often as I need to in order to learn what I need to learn from that situation. Often life gives us similar situations over and over again to give us good opportunity to learn what we need to learn to "get over" or see through a habitual pattern. That is part of why connecting through generosity is so powerful: in this act, we "get over" ourselves and begin to tear down our walls.

Once I have banged into that wall enough that I have learned what I need to learn, it is likely that – rather than indignation, frustration, anger, self-righteousness, whatever it is – I will be able to bring to the situation patience, compassion and kindness. This is the sign I am getting ready to drop my stick.

Be patient, and offer the whole thing kindness? It will take the air right out of those tires.

So, touch in with our bigness. Then, wield the sword, the power of our discernment, to cut through the appearance to the space and freedom that lies on the other side. Like Indra, we will have set the sun in the sky and caused the waters of abundance and delight to flow.

Can we distinguish between the true and the false?

Our limits are the beginning and the end simultaneously. They give us our life and our death. They are the gateway to freedom from suffering....because they give us our suffering.

How otherwise would we be inspired to change? They are how we wake ourselves up.

I am illustrating it in relation to a person. The same would be true in relation to a medical situation or other situation where the hard thing is not a person. Take a deep breath. Touch into space. Then wield the strength of your insight, intelligence and discernment: you will be able to see how you need to handle it or what you need to do.

Fight against it, resist it (oh, it is so hot), and the experience of it as the enemy will build: very good! There will be more to fight against, more to push against. If we welcome the experience (I am so grateful for the fan beside my desk. Most people have to pay to have a sauna...) then with that patience, and in that cradle of kindness, the experience of separateness will relax, and we will see through it. We will cut through it. There will be relief, release and space. We will have overcome the obstacle and become stronger for it.

The invitation is to be the hero in our own lives. Wield the courage and the strength of our insight by relaxing into space. How I work with it doesn't matter. Push against, or welcome it and let it go: I win either way. It is *that* I work with it that matters: that makes me the hero of my own story.

That is how we get born: we push against; we get squeezed; we push against. That is what it is like to move through a birth canal. It is hard and uncomfortable; it's painful. It is not all bad, and it is for something. Pushing is how we continue to be reborn, in the course of our lives: shifting, and changing, and growing into our most authentic and genuine selves.

Are you the hero of your own story?

Touch in with your deep strength, then wield your own sword of awareness and insight. Each time we let go, in this act of re-birthing ourselves - which is what it is to grow and evolve - part of our self-concept dies. We gradually return home to our natural state, but, as the journey continues, we do leave in the past the person we once were.

That is part of the reason why it can be hard to let go.

Do we grieve the loss of the relationship, or do we grieve the loss of the person that we knew ourselves to be in that relationship? Do we grieve not the loss of the past situation, but the loss of the familiarity we had in that situation that was so comfortable to us? Our habitual suffering is familiar, even if it is painful.

It once happened that I unexpectedly went for a hike with a friend in a valley perhaps a half hour drive north from where I was living at that time. I hadn't anticipated the hike. I wasn't wearing the proper shoes. I was wearing a kind of sandal that would slip and slide about, and my foot was always at risk of coming out of the shoe. It was a wonderful hike, but, at some point, I ended up in quite a sandy, steep incline, going up that hill with my feet slipping and sliding in their shoes. So I had the instinct to reach out and hold on. I held on to what was closest that appeared to be stable, certain, reliable, hold-on-to-able.

Without even seeing that I was doing it, I started to steady myself by holding on to rose bushes, with the thorns coming into my hand as I held on, moving from one rose bush to the next.

My friend actually did have to point out to me what it was that I was doing, and it didn't take me so long to observe that the grasses growing out of the hill - that I could hold onto as easily as if I was holding onto the mane of a horse - were much steadier, much stronger, and much more deeply rooted....and they came without thorns.

To step into the authentic presence of what our genuine self truly is - step by step – is to gradually let go of those things that we hold onto that cause us our suffering. We gradually leave some part of our smallness behind: it becomes victory over war.

We don't need to be our own worst enemy.

Meditation practice is sometimes compared to the training of a horse. The untrained mind - with thoughts, and emotions, and fears, and pain that it doesn't understand how to work with - can buck and thrash about like an untrained horse, so that we are not riding the horse. We are being thrashed about. We are being ridden by it.

The potential and power of the horse is beyond measure, but to beat the horse into submission is unhelpful. We don't need to constantly recite the litany of our supposed unworthiness and inadequacy. A horse whisperer approach is recommended.

You are enough. You are part of the planet like the sand on the beach and the stars in the sky. That's enough. Simply that you are breathing makes it enough.

As we learn to accompany ourselves on the journey, and return to that part of ourselves that we know to be genuine and true, we gently welcome the horse, welcome the mind, home.

Step 2: Engage the Journey

The journey to engage our lives, in an aware, meaningful, purposeful way can sometimes be compared to spiritual warriorship. It can require the courage of a soldier to be able to own the strength of one's own human potential and to genuinely wield an authentic personal power.

In this worldview associated with the mindfulness practices, however, to engage the journey of our lives in an aware, deep and meaningful way is the purpose of our lives. The dare is to not seek to escape from our own experience. Can we rather accompany ourselves and be where we are when we're there?

The purpose of our lives is to live.

Like the plants and the trees, we, too, are organic. As our life process unfolds, often it is what we most need that presents itself to us: not necessarily what we most want, but rather what we most need.

Understand our experience as helping us to open and unfold deeply to our human potential, and our lives become a container for us to grow in wisdom, strength, insight and courage, more deeply connected to that inherent nature of mind – strong, kind and wise - that we already are.

Joseph Campbell, in his work on the mytheme of the hero's quest in world culture – work which inspired George Lucas to create the Star Wars series - shows that essentially all founders of our religious traditions, as ones who bear witness to human greatness, can be considered spiritual heroes or spiritual warriors. It is likely I could illustrate this in relation, for example, to Jesus of Nazareth, Moses, Muhammad or others.

The historic Buddha, Siddhartha Gautama, is understood in the tradition - a non-theistic tradition – as a human model of what is possible for the human experience. The tradition itself understands it in this way.

So let me illustrate this quality of engaging the journey by telling you his story. His life story is told in Buddhist tradition in order to offer those who follow him, in subsequent generations of spiritual seekers, a map. How do we undertake the journey home?

The word "Buddha" means awakened one or enlightened one. It is derived from BUDH-, meaning to "wake up": to wake up spiritually, to wake up to a different perception of reality.

In the same way that when we wake from a dreaming state we can say, "Ah, I was sleeping. Now I am awake.", when we "wake up" in the sense of enlightenment we will look back on our everyday relative existence -thinking small things are big things, thinking the self is a solid - and say, "Ah, I was asleep. Now I am awake."

"Buddha" is an honorary title ascribed to one who is recognized as having woken up in this way. It is, therefore, a title in the way that "Dr." or "Reverand" is an honorary title.

The historic Buddha, Siddhartha Gautama, was born the son of the King Suddhodana, ruler of the Kingdom of the Sakyas, with his capital near Kapilavastu in modern Southern Nepal. His father called him Siddhartha, which means "wish-fulfilling", because he fulfilled the long cherished wish of the barren royal family that there would be a son who could inherent the throne, and because at the time of his birth many blessings and much prosperity had come to the land.

Seven days after he was born, the story goes, his mother died, leaving him under the care of her sister, Mahaprajapati, who would eventually play an important role in the development of the Buddhist order of nuns. It is said that on the sixth day of his life, Siddartha was taken to the astrologers, as would be considered common, perhaps even normal, in Indian culture even today.

The astrologer said to the King, "Oh, Your Majesty your son is magnificent! He will either be a great king and great ruler of your kingdom, or, if he is exposed to signs of human suffering - old age, sickness, or death - he will renounce the life of royalty, and become a great spiritual leader."

The King needed to have a successor to the kingdom, and so the prince grew up surrounded by abundance, and pleasure, and beauty in order that he would never see the suffering of life. When he was sixteen, his father feared he might become dissatisfied, and gave him in marriage to a young maiden said to be the most beautiful in the land.

This part of the story of the map of the human experience of growing up to our spiritual potential does show us that it is considered a natural part of this organic process that there may be a time in our lives when the material things, and sensual pleasures, seem to be sufficient, and we find a relative contentment in these things. So the material things, and sensual pleasures, are understood to be neither good nor bad, and there is a time in the process of our personal growth when the seeking of these things has its own kind of sufficiency, and brings its own kind of fulfilment.

Siddhartha would come to a time when he experienced that the golden cage of his palace - where every material and sensual need was being met -was still a cage. He longed to see what life was like outside of these palace walls.

So it happened one night that he covered himself in a cloak, so no one would see who he was. He went with his chariot driver outside the gates of the palace, and he saw an old man by the side of the road: hunched over, and gray, limping with a cane, moving slowly, and in pain. Gautama said, "What is it that!". "That is old age, Sir." "Does every one grow old?". "Yes, everyone grows old, Sir." "Will I grow old?". "Yes, you, too, will grow old, Sir."

Another night, dressed in the cloak, he went outside of the palace walls. He saw a sick person by the side of the road, surrounded by his own filth. He said to his chariot driver, "What is that?". "That is sickness, Sir". "Does everyone get sick?". "Yes, everyone gets sick, Sir." "Will I get sick? "Yes, one day you, too, will become sick, Sir."

A third night, dressed in his cloak, he went outside of the palace walls. He saw a corpse lying by the side of the road. He said to his chariot driver, "What is that!!". "That is death, Sir."

"Does everyone die?". "Yes, everyone dies, Sir." "Will I also die?". "Yes, you will also die, Sir."

An insatiable longing arose inside of him to engage the journey: there must be a way to find freedom from suffering.

This is a step on the journey. Many people find, when they are confronted by a strong hardship in their lives - the death of someone they love, sickness for themselves or someone they love, perhaps one of their children is suffering or in pain, maybe a child has watched a parent suffering or in pain - some strong, life-changing incident happens, and suddenly the "stuff" feels hollow.

The sensory distractions, the sensory pleasures, somehow don't seem to touch us anymore, and the whole thing becomes, in some way, not enough. So we engage the journey. We engage the quest: "Is that all there is? It feels hollow and empty. I feel cold, confused and alone. Please, someone, tell me how to find freedom from my suffering. There must be some deeper meaning and purpose for my life. This can't be all that there, is this hollow, empty world of plastic and stuff."

At the time of the birth of his own son, when he had provided succession to the throne, and with the support of his wife, on the full moon day of the month of May, he secretly left his home, took off his royal clothes, and took the clothes of a wandering spiritual seeker. For six years, he wandered, sometimes in groups and sometimes alone.

He practiced extreme spiritual practices, extreme yoga, extreme fasting, denying himself food until he was only a skeleton, and one day he fell into a faint. He concluded, "It's not so useful, to practice extreme fasting until I fall into a faint!". He would establish a principle known as "the middle way", a core part of the pathway that he would trace.

He felt that the extreme luxury, the extreme abundance and sensory pleasure that he had, was not so useful for his spiritual seeking, because it was possible to get lost in it. He felt that the extreme fasting, the extreme yoga practice - fasting until he was a skeleton, essentially transparent, and would fall into a faint - was also exaggerated and unhelpful. It's not possible to meditate if you've fallen into a faint.

He would begin to trace this quality of the "middle way": not too tight, not to loose, not utterly rejecting the material world, or but not being consumed by it either.

It was a on full moon day of the month of May, when he was 35 years old, that he received a nourishing bowl of food from a woman named Sujata, who would become an important early donor in Buddhist tradition.

Sujata was wealthy, and there had been a time when she was longing to have a son. The villagers had told her that she should go to pray to the tree god and ask that she be granted a son. So she went to pray to the tree god, and she was granted a son. She had prepared a very, sweet nourishing bowl of milk rice, rather like a milk pudding, and she had placed it in a golden bowl to take it to the tree god as an offering.

What matters is that it was a bowl of food, that was warm, nourishing and comforting. So you will visualize what that food is like for you. Is it a dish of rice pudding? Tibetan culture has a sweet, sticky rice that has dried fruit and nuts in it. There are cultures where rice isn't commonly eaten. It might be hard for you to imagine a bowl of rice pudding, so you will imagine what is warm, comforting and nourishing for you. I once offered this story to someone, and we decided that, for her, it would be a warm and nourishing plate of lasagna; she had enjoyed lasagna at a family feast just a day or two before.

Sujata brought this golden bowl of food wishing to offer it to the tree god, and she found - sitting at the base of this tree - what did appear to be a tree god. He was so skinny and frail. You could see all of his bones. His skin was shiny and somehow transparent. Gautama received the bowl from Sujata, who said to him, "May you be successful in obtaining your wishes, just as I have been."

So, he ate this nourishing food, and he sat down at the base of the tree, which is now known as the Bodhi tree, or the tree of awakening. It is possible to visit that Bodhi tree in a place called Bodh Gaya in the Indian state of Bihar. It's now an important place of pilgrimage.

He sat down at the base of the tree, and he said, "Let my skin, my sinews and my bones dry up, and likewise my flesh and my blood, but until I have attained the Supreme Enlightenment, *I will not leave this posture!*".

The decision, and it is sometimes a decision like that, is when we engage the journey. The decision will tend to be very similar, regardless of what the journey looks like for you. So let me offer this suggestion. One day, you make the decision to make some strong change in your life. You're going to go back to school. You're going to quit smoking. You're going to start jogging.

You're going to eat in a way which nourishes you more fully. Maybe it's a decision to do less of something. Maybe its choosing to have a life which is different from the people that have surrounded me, because I feel like, if I have a lifestyle like theirs, it will take me to a place that I don't want to go.

Whatever it is for you, when you come to a point of making a decision like that in your life, make the decision, with the clarity and the finality that we're seeing illustrated in the story here. I will go back to school. I will get the training I need to be able to change jobs, so I can have a job which feels like it has meaning and purpose to me.

First, make the decision. Then, don't tell anyone. Do not post it to social media. You decide you're going to engage with exercise in your life in a new kind of way, because you feel that will increase your vitality, vigor and joyfulness. You decide, then you don't tell anyone. The people around you have a concept of you. They love you just the way you are, or rather they love you in the way they have the habit of seeing you, either consciously or not. If you begin to step outside the boundaries of their concept of you, they will seek to return you to the way you were before, because they are comfortable with you in that way.

Maybe the people in your world really do see you and know you as you are. Perhaps you are in a situation where you can reach out with the baby seed of a wish to do or be something new and be seen, and heard, and met in celebration of that.

Often, however, you change and grow outside the boundaries of their concept of you, and you challenge in some way their concept of themselves. This can make people uncomfortable.

They will seek to return you to the familiar, unless, of course you, feel with strong confidence that they are ready to leap with you. This is possible, sometimes.

Be aware that often humans in relationship can function a bit like crabs. I am told that when fisher-people fish for crab, they only need to use a box that is a very small number of inches high. Any crab would be able to crawl out of that box, but it's not a problem for the fisher-people: any time one crab tries to crawl out of that box, the other crab will pull it back in.

To engage the journey can mean making choices that the people around you may not anticipate or expect. They may need time to recognise change has occurred. It can take up to a year for the concept of "me" that people around me are holding to change. It's my experience that you could probably get another university degree, increase your income by a hundred thousand dollars, drop fifty pounds, and sail around the world in a one person yacht, and they may still not notice the difference. There is freedom in the space in-between your decision to make the change and their noticing – sometime later – that the change has already taken place.

They're wearing their visor. It can be hard for people's concepts to change. Information to the contrary of the concept gets filtered out. Consider if it may be useful for you to make a decision about a strong life change that, like Mary of Nazareth, you might keep to yourself and ponder in your heart.

You can be brave enough to let yourself discover what the potential might be for you as a person. You have permission to let your magnificence fly free.

Gautama sat at the base of the tree. He made the decision, and something tells me he must have said it out loud, for all through the night, we are told, he was tempted. "Aren't your legs getting stiff and sore? Wouldn't you like to get up and have a stretch? I wonder how much your son has grown since last you saw him? I wonder if your son even remembers what you look like? I bet that beautiful wife of yours has gotten together with someone else by now…. Wouldn't you like to go home to your wife?".

It is said that all through the night he was tempted. He remained resolute and strong. When the morning came, he had attained enlightenment.

We are told that he sat under the tree for seven more days, looking at the patterns: contemplating the nature of cause and effect and the impermanence and fleeting change of things. We are told he had no intention to teach. How could anyone possibly understand?

It was his instinct to be quiet, but then it happened that some people, who had been practicing with him earlier, came upon him in the forest, and they saw the difference in him. "What happened to you?", they said.

We are told he touched the earth, in what is called the Earth-touching "mudra". "With the earth as my witness", he said, "I have attained enlightenment. I have woken up."

His former companions asked him to teach. This remains an important part of Buddhist tradition. A teacher will only teach in response to a request for teachings. People might have travelled from all over the world to fill a football stadium to be able to receive the teachings from a high teacher. There will still be a formal request for teachings, and the high teacher will give teachings only after that person has been requested to do so.

If more deeply engaging in mindfulness practice is among the life changing decisions you are considering, I offer the respectful observation that all wisdom traditions in my awareness share a very similar attitude. It is quite humble. It communicates more in its silence than it does in its sound.

Buddhism is not a missionary tradition. One traditional metaphor is the "upside down teacup": try to pour the teachings into the mind of someone who is closed - and not wanting to receive the teachings - and you might as well try to pour tea into an upside down teacup.

If you wish to deepen your connection with yourself and others through your own mindfulness practice, a very good away to inspire other people to do the same is through example. Be more patient, more gentle, more kind, more strong, and more wise. Maybe they will simply come to more deeply enjoy your companionship. Perhaps one day, they might ask for teachings, but do not long for that day, and let them ask.

The Buddha received the request for teachings. For the rest of his 80 years of life, he taught his followers until the time of his "parinirvana", his transition out of that human body, the same day he was born, the same day of his enlightenment, the full moon day of the month of May.

His early teachings would build on those observations that he had in those seven days of sitting under the tree. The self is not a solid. Things are not permanent. Things shift and change, like the movement of molecules would appear under a very sensitive microscope that sees that the things that appear to be solid are actually shifting and moving all the time.

He would offer his first teachings in a place that is known as Deer Park. Even today the deer gather where the teachings are practiced and taught. I've been to retreat centers in Colorado where I felt like the deer might line up with the rest of us for morning coffee and breakfast. They didn't line up for coffee, but they were seen to walk among people in the courtyard, and they were found seated on the other side of the glass of the windows of the shrine room where people were practicing meditation.

At the Buddhist monastery in Cape Breton that I've mentioned, it was more a question of moose. National Park officials have intentionally lowered the number of moose in the area as part of their stewardship of that land, but I have lived at the Abbey at a time when keeping the moose out of the garden was getting people's attention.

One day, I had morning coffee and breakfast sitting on the stone bench in the garden about 15 feet away from a moose, who was nibbling at leaves on a tree, having breakfast beside me. Where meditation is happening, somehow the deer seem to be sensitive to it. They are curious and interested, and they come. They somehow instinctively know that these humans will not cause harm.

In these early Deer Park teachings, Gautama sought to answer the question that he was asked, "how do we find freedom from our suffering?". He answered the question in what is now known as the Four Noble Truths.

The Four Noble Truths are given according to the formulaic pattern of ancient Indian medical prescriptions. Visit an Ayurvedic, or ancient Indian doctor of Gautama's time, and that doctor would give a prescription like this. What is the symptom of the problem? What is the root cause of the problem? What is the root solution to the problem? How do we apply that root solution?

That it is because we understand that the basic nature of the body is to be healthy that we know how to recognize sickness, and we go to a doctor to get medicine that will help to heal the sickness. Because health is the basic state of the body, the body will do everything in its power to return to a state of health.

In the same way, the basic nature of the mind is to be content, to experience a relative sense of peace and satisfaction. If it were not so, it would not feel like there is something wrong when we become upset, or angry, or begin to cry. It is because we know that contentment is possible- natural and normal - that we look for solutions to try to find freedom from our suffering.

Gautama would ask: "what is the problem?". In the course of our lives, we experience different kinds of suffering. It's not that all of being alive is suffering, but that in the course of a human life, there will be the suffering of being born, the suffering of being sick, the suffering of aging, the suffering of witnessing the death of the people around us, and the suffering of our own death. To have something or be in a situation we dislike is suffering; to have something or be in a situation where we're separated from what we do like is suffering; to not get what we want is a kind of suffering.

More formally, the tradition describes three kinds of suffering. The first is the "suffering of suffering". This is entry level, "stub your toe", kind of suffering. You cut your finger. You get angry. It is the day-to-day suffering we experience, with our everyday bodies, in our everyday worlds. If you have a finger, from time to time, you will get a sliver in that finger. This kind of "from time to time" suffering is entered in the general category: the "suffering of suffering".

The next level of subtlety of understanding suffering is called the "suffering of change". If you are feeling good in a situation, it is just the nature of things that the situation, and you, will change. If you are feeling bad about a situation, it is the nature of things that, eventually, the situation, and you will change. The act of the change, losing the familiar, is registered by the mind as a kind of suffering. The mind can be quite conditioned to be comfortable with its habits, even if those habits are causing us pain.

The third kind of suffering is the most subtle of the three, and this is the awareness - at some dark, back, dusty, cobwebby corner of our mind - that things really aren't as solid as they appear. The whole thing really is like a dream. We spend our lives being fussed and bothered by these things which are designed to help us to grow as persons, help us to ripen, to draw out those deep qualities that are the potential for the human experience, and somehow at the end of the journey, we arrive where we started and realize that none of it was real in the first place. It's just like that wolf that was only a rock, and suddenly we notice "wolflessness". So that dusty, dark, back corner of our minds will struggle, trying to manufacture a self that is solid, and real, even though - in some way - it knows that it's not. There was never a self there in the first place.

The first of the Four Noble Truths: what is the surface symptom of the problem? In the course of a human life, we experience suffering, not as a solid or constant state, but it comes, and it goes, in the way that days cycle into nights, and clouds move through the sky. So, how do we work with it when it happens?

Noble truth number two: what is the root cause of our suffering? We cause ourselves suffering when we try to hold on to the self – or our "self-concept" as if it were solid, or we hold onto something in the outside world that we think is going to make us happy. We hold on, almost like holding ourselves up with the rosebushes. "If only he responds to my text message, then I'll be happy". "If only...". What gets put in that blank changes moment to moment. It is the instinct that says something is wrong, and something out there will fix it. I will either get what I like, or push away what I don't like, or ignore what I can't really handle, but something out there is the answer.

What is the root solution to the problem? Noble Truth, number three: stop grasping. Let go. Stop holding yourself up with rose bushes. Give yourself the space you need to notice that what you are looking for, you already have. You are sufficient. You are enough. There is absence of absence. This is the gateway to satisfaction, contentment, creativity, vitality, abundance and delight.

Noble Truth four: how do we do that? Engage the journey.

How these people would apply the teachings is what we now call Buddhist psychology and philosophy. It is just the record of these people's experience of witnessing the mind. It created a way for this experience to be communicated from one generation to the next for over 2500 years.

When Gautama was giving his first public teaching, however, he was not talking to Buddhists: there were no Buddhists yet! He was just talking to people who wanted to find good ways to work with suffering, to find freedom from suffering: not that there won't be hard things in our lives afterwards – sure there will be – but we will be able to relate to them in a way that makes us stronger, like the muscle at the gym. We tear the muscle fibers slightly at the gym in order that they grow back stronger.

The very convenient thing about the mind is that we take it with us wherever we go. We take ourselves with us wherever we go. So, we can work with the mind in any context. Any situation we are in – any path of mastery we are exploring – can become the mirror for the mind.

If you are an athlete, apply it to athletics.

If you are an artist, apply it to art.

It you are a parent, apply it to parenting.

If you are a student, bring it with you into your residence and into your papers and exams.

Take a deep breath. Gather your inner winds. Then, engage your insight, awareness, intelligence and courage....and go!!

You are the hero in your own life.

The mindfulness practices are ways to notice what is happening with the patterns of thoughts in the mind or patterns of emotions in our experience. It is a way of becoming familiar with the mind. The Tibetan word used to name the rectangular cushion used as a meditation seat is: "gomden". "Gomden" means "to become familiar". This is part of what meditation practice is. Can we become more familiar with the mirror that is the mind, and more discerning of the difference between the true and the false, the fake and the real? What we will choose to accept in our lives, and what will we choose to reject?

You may choose to engage the path, the journey of our lives, in this deeper, thoughtful and more meaningful way. Once you start, it doesn't stop. Life becomes the journey of discovery. It is rich and meaningful, but it is not always easy.

Then, if you wish, look at the choices you are making in our lives in the outside world. It is called "creating the practice container". Behave in a way in relation to the outside world that is stable, and basically healthy, and basically sane enough that the mind is not constantly being disturbed at the same time that it is learning how to relax. It relates to both how we treat others and how we treat ourselves.

Act because you want the effect of the cause. Do not be seduced by what you like or don't like – or choose to ignore - in the short term. What we feel is good or bad for us – what we accept and what we reject in our lives – will likely shift and change over time just as we do. Ask yourself: is it skillful, or is it not skillful? Will it take me where I want or need to go, or not? Then, choose the skillful.

Speak and act, in relation to ourselves and others, in ways that pay close attention to ensure that you will not cause harm.

Remember the boomerang effect: what I offer the world will, in some way, will come back to me. There is nowhere for it to go. Choose a way to make your living that does not cause harm, to yourself or to other beings. It makes it hard for the mind to relax if one's behavior in the outside world consistently causes it to be disturbed.

This forms the basis of Buddhist ethics. The basis of the ethics is similar in every culture in my awareness. First, do no harm. Then, when you have that as a relatively stable work in progress, be of benefit to others. Benefit beings in as open-hearted and genuine a way as possible. The traditional list of how to benefit beings is: generosity, discipline, patience, exertion, training the stability of the mind through meditation, and consistently growing in one's ability for awareness of self and other so that we develop wisdom. This puts in place what we need to then begin to truly work with the mind itself.

Apply exertion: not too tight but not too loose. Just like training at the gym, be regular enough to slowly get stronger. Begin with the possible. Celebrate successes, however large or small they may be.

Then, engage the mindfulness practices, growing in the strength, relaxation and stability that is a fundamental and inherent aspect of the mind. Engage the mindfulness practice to also foster the mind's ability for insight, awareness and wisdom. Many people do "shamatha-vipashyana" which is "calm abiding" and "awareness" practice: it trains both of these inherent abilities of the mind.

Often we are supported in this by having models or examples of people, in some way in our lives, that can serve as an inspiration and a guide.

Often we are supported in this by engaging the journey in community, with other seekers on the path to a good, decent, meaningful and engaged, fulfilling life.

Push against or welcome. It is both this and that: either way we win.

If you engage the journey, then you participate in your life. It is no longer something that happens to you. You participate in that flow of the life force that "flows together", in the cycle of life, shaping your nights and your days.

The journey is impersonal in the sense that whatever the vehicle is that supports our discovery of our genuineness, that is a vehicle that will support us in our discovery of our potential and our genuineness. Engage that.

I know someone who engages the journey by being a race car driver, and that becomes the mirror and metaphor that shows him his edges, and helps to push him beyond his limits. Whatever the metaphor is for you, know that it is a very multi-purpose mirror, and any situation where we find ourselves can show us a reflection of ourselves, because it is all part of the broader nature of mind.

The mindfulness practices are designed to help the mind to slow down so that it can better bear witness to its own experience and better identify its own patterns. You may wish to integrate mindfulness practice of some kind into your life. Remember, too, that it is the space in-between where life is. Seek to make a regular habit of booking time for yourself for self-care. Offer yourself honour and respect, as we accompany ourselves in our lives.

Step 3: Build Your Strength

When we train the body at the gym, we are working to tear down the muscle fibres slightly so that when they grow back they will become stronger. The mind really is like that. As we engage the journey, working with hard things, gradually the mind becomes stronger. The hard things are not the only part of the journey, but they are a part of the journey, and they are part of how we build our strength.

The depth and subtlety of our character is carved by our wounds, and, more precisely, how we work to heal those, and then to let them go.

It can be that it is our wounds that cut the heart open. It may be painful, but is that pain "bad"? Often, pain is not without purpose of some kind, if we are able to work with that situation, with kindness, intelligence, strength and insight.

If it has happened, and it's hard, it is possible for us to work with it to make that pain be for something. If it's hard, let it be for something, so, like those muscles in the gym, we come out of it stronger than we were before.

We might be frustrated by the small things that cause us harm, until there is a bigger hard thing that comes along. Then we work with that bigger hard thing, and engage our intelligence and resourcefulness, so that when we are through it, we are better able to be confident that we have what we need to handle whatever it is that will come to us next.

If there were no hard things, where would be the motivation to connect with, and foster, delight? The strength of our character is carved by our wounds. It is how we become stronger.

I am told that, in Japan, broken objects - like a cracked cup, for example - are often repaired with gold. The flaw is seen as a unique piece of the object's history which adds to its beauty.

We can be broken open by heartbreak.

We grow and change in our ability to work with hard things as individuals. We also grow and change in our ability to work with hard things as a society.

We are one generation away from a time when many things were not spoken aloud, from a time when divorce was unthinkable, and - if a person was in a position of unsafety or abuse, a family member was alcoholic - it was not socially acceptable to talk about those hard things, or to actively seek to find a way out. We are maybe two generations away from a time when many women did not have independent income, for example, and therefore they had fewer choices in terms of what to accept and to what to reject in the course of their own lives.

As a culture, it was perhaps through the 1980's and 1990's when publicly speaking about hard things became socially normalized. Perhaps the very public divorce, for example, between the late Princess Diana and Charles, Prince of Wales is an example of this. Where once the suffering would have been with the silence of that British war motto "keep calm and carry on" - keep your head down, and your mouth closed, and just handle it - we moved into a time where people began to speak openly, and publicly, about hard things and wounds.

To be able to give voice to hard things was an important social step and has opened social conversation to now more actively include, for example, questions of gender identity, or sexual preference, or respect and reconciliation for First Nations communities.

I feel there is room for us to continue to grow and develop in the public discourse that we are using as we cope, together, with hard things.

Sometimes an experience is so intensely hard that it burns itself into us like a tattoo, searing us to the core, provoking years of healing. We can go through times when it is important to receive the social space to be heard saying: I am a victim of this or that; I was abused in this way or that; there was treachery in this way or that. The healing journey can be so long, we can forget what health feels like. If it becomes too solid – a strong part of our identity – it risks to get stuck, and then to fester under the skin. To hold on to it – to get stuck with it – is, in some way, to be trapped. We will harvest the strength we earn from this only after we let go.

There is a renovation and construction happening on the university campus where I teach. New buildings are being built, and an old building is being quite strongly renovated.

It means that all of us who had offices in that older building needed to vacate the space. The building was going to be stripped down all the way to the brick. In the course of the big move, as we packed up generations, it seemed, of books out of that building, several of us agreed that we had to save the aloe vera plant in the stairwell.

It was the largest aloe vera plant that any of us had ever encountered, and it had just too much character and spirit: it could not be left behind.

I ended up being the one who adopted the aloe vera plant. It was no small feat. It was so heavy that it was moved by the professional movers who helped us in the process of vacating this office tower. When it moved into my kitchen, it had a prehistoric dinosaur quality to it: I felt like I should move out, because I was living in someone else's space.

It took me more than ten days to work up my courage to repot this plant. It was obviously suffering in a container far too small. Having gathered my courage, I did one day bring the tool box upstairs. It took a hammer - loud, long, repeat applications of the hammer - to break the terracotta pot that the roots of the plant had been fighting against for so long.

When the pot was finally shattered into bits, I was able to see that - back all those years ago, when someone had planted that plant - they had made a decision that it would be good to save on the cost of potting soil. They had put a smaller plastic plant pot upside down underneath, in order that the pot would take less soil...and the roots of the plant would be forced to grow around that great empty hollow space of the plastic underneath.

If I have a wound that is so strong that I don't know how to let go of it, and if I engage that wound in such a way that it becomes fixed as part of my identity - and in some way I have self-defined as a victim of some sort - in my experience, it can be like that hollow, empty, plastic space underneath, where no roots can grow, and there is no nourishment available, no soil available where there should be. It can be hard on the outside, and hollow and empty on the inside.

All journeys are worthy of respect. Any change and growth happens in its own time. Those of us who feel we may have been victimized, as it were, surely have very good reason to feel that way.

I would wish for us, though, when the time is right, that we will be able to break that pot that is too small for us, that we are being squeezed into, and take away that great, hollow, empty, plastic space inside, and make it right again.

The plant got brand new soil and a brand new pot. I think he would like a bigger pot; I just don't know where to find one. He needs to have a terracotta pot of the kind that can breathe. One day, I'll find him one.

I took a hacksaw that day and used the hacksaw to cut off the old and dead branches, and - perhaps it's a bit like those thorns on the rose bush – it never occurred to me that perhaps I should be wearing gloves as I hacked off with the hacksaw these very large, thick, perhaps three inch diameter dead branches. It did, actually, leave fine lasting scars.

May my scars heal.

May all of our scars heal.

May any of us who are feeling hollowed out, and cold, and somehow unnourished and unfed, be cared for, and held, and nourished and fed.

There are now new baby aloe vera plants growing beside those older branches, and new life is coming from those wounds.

Conclusion

*"Beyond the enemy,
there is magic."*
-Adela.

Buddhism enters the region known as Tibet in about the year 1000. It will arrive there at the request of a king of Tibet who wanted his communities to be able to live together in a healthier and good way. He wanted to create an enlightened society, where people would live together in a way that would have kindness as its point of reference instead of aggression or fear.

When Buddhism moved from India into Tibet, it would join with the shamanic culture known as "bon" which had been in the area from very early times. This old shamanic culture had strong appreciation for what it was to live in the highest region of the world: the sharp spikes of the mountains; the roar of the wind; the shadows cast on the snow. They lived close enough to the natural elements that the elements themselves began to feel alive. The water inside the body, and the water of the snow, or the warmth of the body, and the warmth of the sun, would blur together slightly, and things felt alive. The elemental world and the human world interacted with a spirit world as part of this experience of being alive.

The Tibetan word used to name this community of the spirit world is "drala". It can refer to the community of the spirits as a collective, "the drala". Perhaps it is in some way comparable to how Jewish, Christian and Islamic traditions recognise the presence of angels. Just because you may have never spoken with one, doesn't mean they don't exist. It's part of what can get filtered out by our visors.

The word "drala", when rendered into English, means literally "beyond the enemy", beyond the limited boundaries of the conceptual mind, and beyond the sense of a self that can move between being more relaxed and more solid as we shift in our experience of walking together as friends, and pushing away as enemies, these qualities of ourselves that we may like or dislike, ignore or find neutral. In this old Tibetan world, it was understood that beyond the enemy, there is magic, and somehow we become more truly alive.

In what sense is it beyond the enemy?

This place of magic, where we are held, protected and blessed, is the space the mind relaxes into that is that same 99.999% of anything that ever was, or ever will be, every grain of sand on the beach, every star in the sky.

That's where contentment is, and satisfaction, genuine creativity, therefore, genuine achievement, the humor and the delight, the love, the friendship, the warmth and gentleness, the kind safety of space.

Buddhism moves from India to the north following the Silk Route; it would make its way into Japan. It would join there with Shinto tradition, and create what is now called Zen Buddhism.

In the art of Zen flower arranging, one might take a very elegant and simple container. Maybe it is something in black metal, rectangular and flat. We add a large branch toward the vertical, not the sharpness of a straight vertical, but something that would curve like the curvature of the sky. We take another branch that lies along the horizontal, perhaps not entirely flat, but something in texture that moves slightly, with contours like the earth. In the middle, we place a flower or perhaps two: some colour, but it is simple. The form is known in Zen flower arranging as heaven, earth and human, or, more traditionally, heaven, earth and man.

It's not about showing us the flower or the branches. The branches and the flower - defining heaven, earth and the space in-between - are all there to help us see space, a space in-between in which we all live.

May you rest in a space between the action of the days, so that your rests, and your notes, will make music of your life, and may the journey bring you joy.

You are enough.

ADELA SANDNESS

Also by this Author

*Mindfulness:
How to Cope with Hard Things,
A Workbook*

ADELA SANDNESS

Adela Sandness holds a Ph.D. from the École Pratique des Hautes Études of the Sorbonne in Paris where she studied ancient Indian, or Vedic, cosmology and, in particular, the goddess Sarasvatī. She is a professor at St. Francis Xavier University in Nova Scotia, Canada, where she teaches mindfulness, Hinduism, Buddhism and aspects of modern Indian experience. Having served for over a decade in leadership roles in mindfulness practice communities, including two years of practice living in a Buddhist monastery, she brings ancient wisdom and her depth of practice experience - along with stories, humor, compassion, care, and a healthy dose of common sense - to help us rediscover ourselves and our relationships and re-think together today's world. Come find her at Just Breathe....You are Enough™: in weekly podcasts, on Instagram, Facebook and Twitter, and at justbreatheyouareenough.com.

www.ingramcontent.com/pod-product-compliance
Lightning Source LLC
Chambersburg PA
CBHW051805040426
42446CB00007B/528